100 WALKS IN
NORTHUMBERLAND

THE CROWOOD PRESS

First published in 2017 by
The Crowood Press Ltd
Ramsbury, Marlborough
Wiltshire SN8 2HR

enquiries@crowood.com

www.crowood.com

This impression 2021

British Library Cataloguing-in-Publication Data
A catalogue record for this book is available from the British Library.

ISBN 978 1 78500 183 3

Mapping in this book is sourced from Google Earth.

Every effort has been made to ensure the accuracy of this book. However, changes can occur
during the lifetime of an edition. The Publishers cannot be held responsible for any errors or
omissions or for the consequences of any reliance on the information given in this book, but
should be very grateful if walkers could let us know of any inaccuracies by writing to us at
the address above or via the website.

As with any outdoor activity, accidents and injury can occur. We strongly advise readers to
check the local weather forecast before setting out and to take an OS map. The Publishers
accept no responsibility for any injuries which may occur in relation to following the walk
descriptions contained within this book.

Typeset by Jean Cussons Typesetting, Diss, Norfolk
Printed and bound in India by Replika Press Pvt. Ltd.

Contents

How to Use this Book   6

Walks Locator   7

WALK 1	Falstone Circular	3 miles (4.8km)	8
WALK 2	Hareshaw Linn	3 miles (4.8km)	10
WALK 3	Walltown to the Milecastle Inn	3 miles (4.8km)	12
WALK 4	Blanchland & Pennypie	3½ miles (5.6km)	14
WALK 5	Druridge Bay & Country Park	3½ miles (5.6km)	16
WALK 6	Holystone & Lady's Well	3½ miles (5.6km)	18
WALK 7	Kilham Hill Trail	3½ miles (5.6km)	20
WALK 8	Steel Rigg & Hotbank	3½ miles (5.6km)	22
WALK 9	Vindolanda & Henshaw	3½ miles (5.6km)	24
WALK 10	Wooler & Earle Mill	3½ miles (5.6km)	26
WALK 11	Housesteads & the Pennine Way	3¾ miles (6km)	28
WALK 12	Sinderhope & the Golf Course	3¾ miles (6km)	30
WALK 13	West Hill & St Gregory's Hill	3¾ miles (6km)	32
WALK 14	Allendale Town & The Hope	4 miles (6.4km)	34
WALK 15	Alnmouth, Lesbury & the Coast	4 miles (6.4km)	36
WALK 16	Biddlestone & Singmoor	4 miles (6.4km)	38
WALK 17	Cawfields & Hallpeat Moss	4 miles (6.4km)	40
WALK 18	Cottingwood Common Circular	4 miles (6.4km)	42
WALK 19	Harbottle & Drakes Stone	4 miles (6.4km)	44
WALK 20	Hartside & Linhope Spout	4 miles (6.4km)	46
WALK 21	Holystone & Dove Crag	4 miles (6.4km)	48
WALK 22	Walltown & Thirlwall Castle	4 miles (6.4km)	50
WALK 23	Allendale Town & the River East Allen	4½ miles (7.2km)	52
WALK 24	Berthele's Stone & Hepburn Wood	4½ miles (7.2km)	54
WALK 25	Carey Burn & Broadstruther	4½ miles (7.2km)	56
WALK 26	Happy Valley & North Middleton	4½ miles (7.2km)	58
WALK 27	Craster & Dunstanburgh Castle	4½ miles (7.2km)	60
WALK 28	Craster & Howick Hall	4½ miles (7.2km)	62
WALK 29	Ford Village Circular	4½ miles (7.2km)	64

WALK 30	Hepple & Coquetdale	4½ miles (7.2km)	66
WALK 31	Sinderhope & Low Acton	4½ miles (7.2km)	68
WALK 32	Spartylea & High Knock Shield	4½ miles (7.2km)	70
WALK 33	Walltown & the Vallum	4½ miles (7.2km)	72
WALK 34	Wooler & Weetwood Moor	4½ miles (7.2km)	74
WALK 35	Humbleton Hill & Wooler Common	4¾ miles (7.6km)	76
WALK 36	Holy Island Circular	5 miles (8km)	78
WALK 37	Ros Castle & Ros Hill Wood	5 miles (8km)	80
WALK 38	Simonside Circular	5 miles (8km)	82
WALK 39	Spartylea & Swinhope	5 miles (8km)	84
WALK 40	The Breamish Valley Hill Forts	5 miles (8km)	86
WALK 41	Thrunton Woods & Castle Hill	5 miles (8km)	88
WALK 42	Morpeth & Bothal	5½ miles (9km)	90
WALK 43	Newbiggin, the Wansbeck & the Art Trail	5½ miles (9km)	92
WALK 44	Once Brewed & Winshields Crags	5½ miles (9km)	94
WALK 45	The Harthope Valley & Middleton Old Town	5½ miles (9km)	96
WALK 46	Wooler & Fowberry	5½ miles (9km)	98
WALK 47	Walltown to Once Brewed	6 miles (9.7km)	100
WALK 48	Allen Banks & Staward Peel	6 miles (9.7km)	102
WALK 49	Bolam Lake & Shaftoe Crags	6 miles (9.7km)	104
WALK 50	Cambo & Kirkwelpington	6 miles (9.7km)	106
WALK 51	Haltwhistle & Park Village	6 miles (9.7km)	108
WALK 52	Ingram & Old Fawdon Hill	6 miles (9.7km)	110
WALK 53	Stannington Circular	6 miles (9.7km)	112
WALK 54	The Rothbury Terraces	6 miles (9.7km)	114
WALK 55	Walltown & the Tipalt Burn	6 miles (9.7km)	116
WALK 56	Wylam & Newburn Bridge	6 miles (9.7km)	118
WALK 57	Alnham & the Shepherds' Cairn	6½ miles (10.5km)	120
WALK 58	College Valley & Hethpool Linn	6½ miles (10.5km)	122
WALK 59	Corbridge & Aydon Castle	6½ miles (10.5km)	124
WALK 60	Featherstone Rowfoot & Coanwood Friends Meeting House	6½ miles (10.5km)	126
WALK 61	Flodden Battle Site & Pallinsburn	6½ miles (10.5km)	128
WALK 62	Fourstones & Bridge End	6½ miles (10.5km)	130
WALK 63	Greenleighton & the Fontburn Reservoir	6½ miles (10.5km)	132
WALK 64	Humbleton & Black Law	6½ miles (10.5km)	134
WALK 65	Rothbury & Lordenshaws Hill Fort	6½ miles (10.5km)	136

WALK 66	Rothbury & Wannie Lines	6½ miles (10.5km)	138
WALK 67	Yeavering Bell & the College Burn	6½ miles (10.5km)	140
WALK 68	Guile Point & Return	7 miles (11.3km)	142
WALK 69	Hartburn Glebe & the Wansbeck	7 miles (11.3km)	144
WALK 70	The Five Kings	7 miles (11.3km)	146
WALK 71	Allendale Town, Catton & the River East Allen	7½ miles (12km)	148
WALK 72	Alwinton & Kidlandlee	7½ miles (12km)	150
WALK 73	Clennell & Puncherton	7½ miles (12km)	152
WALK 74	Eglingham, Cateran Hole & Blawearie	7½ miles (12km)	154
WALK 75	Etal & the River Till	7½ miles (12km)	156
WALK 76	Hartside & Little Dod	7½ miles (12km)	158
WALK 77	Hauxley & Amble	7½ miles (12km)	160
WALK 78	Hethpool & the Border Ridge	7½ miles (12km)	162
WALK 79	Humbleton Burn & Hellpath	7½ miles (12km)	164
WALK 80	Once Brewed & Vindolanda	7½ miles (12km)	166
WALK 81	Steel Rigg & Housesteads	7½ miles (12km)	168
WALK 82	Haydon Bridge & the Stublick Chimney	8 miles (13km)	170
WALK 83	Lambley & the South Tyne Trail	8 miles (13km)	172
Walk 84	Morpeth & Mitford	8 miles (13km)	174
WALK 85	Hulne Park Circular	8½ miles (13.7km)	176
WALK 86	The Cheviot	8½ miles (13.7km)	178
WALK 87	Thrunton Woods & Long Crag	8½ miles (14.1km)	180
WALK 88	Blanchland & Slaley Forest	9 miles (14.5km)	182
WALK 89	Blanchland Moor	9 miles (14.5km)	184
WALK 90	Bolam Lake & South Middleton	9 miles (14.5km)	186
WALK 91	Fourstones & the Scout Camp	9 miles (14.5km)	189
WALK 92	Wylam & Horsley	9½ miles (15.3km)	191
WALK 93	Allendale Town & the Chimneys	10 miles (16km)	193
WALK 94	Alwinton & Copper Snout	10 miles (16km)	195
WALK 95	Bamburgh & Glororum	10 miles (16km)	197
WALK 96	Killhope Lead Mining Centre & Allenheads	10 miles (16km)	199
WALK 97	Tom Tallon's Crag	10 miles (16km)	201
WALK 98	Wark & Redesmouth	10 miles (16km)	203
WALK 99	Warkworth & the River Aln	10½ miles (16.9km)	205
WALK 100	Thropton & Tosson Hill	11½ miles (18.5km)	207

How to Use this Book

The walks in the book are ordered by distance, starting with the shortest at
3 miles and ending with the longest at 11½ miles. An information panel for
each walk shows the distance, start point (see below), a summary of level
of difficulty (Easy/Moderate/Hard/Strenuous), OS map(s) required, and
suggested pubs/cafés at the start/end of walk or on the way. An introductory
sentence at the beginning of each walk briefly describes the route and terrain.

Readers should be aware that starting point postcodes have been
supplied for satnav purposes and are not indicative of exact locations. Some
start points are so remote that there is no postcode.

MAPS
There are 100 maps covering the 100 walks.

Start Points
The start of each walk is given as a postcode and also a six-figure grid
reference number prefixed by two letters (which indicates the relevant
square on the National Grid). More information on grid references is found
on Ordnance Survey maps.

Parking
Many of the car parks suggested are public, but for some walks you will have
to park on the roadside or in a lay-by. Please be considerate when leaving
your car and do not block access roads or gates. Also, if parking in a pub car
park for the duration of the walk, please try to avoid busy times.

COUNTRYSIDE CODE
- Consider the local community and other people enjoying the outdoors
- Leave gates and property as you find them and follows paths
- Leave no trace of your visit and take litter home
- Keep dogs under effective control
- Plan ahead and be prepared
- Follow advice and local signs

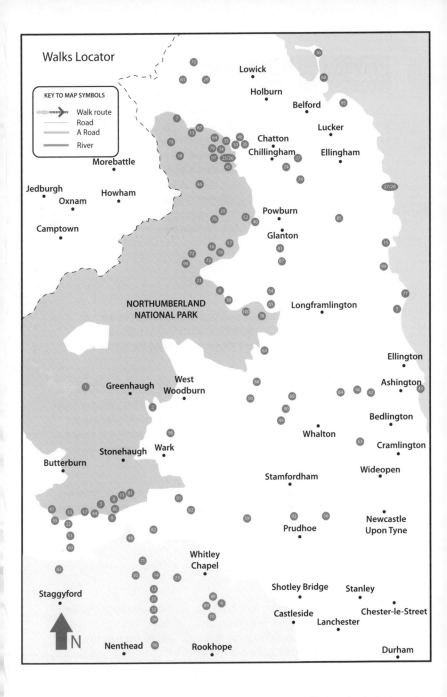

Falstone Circular

START Old School Tea Rooms, Falstone, GR NY723874

NEAREST POSTCODE NE48 1AA

DISTANCE 3 miles (4.8km)

SUMMARY Easy

MAP OS Explorer OL42 Kielder Water & Forest

WHERE TO EAT AND DRINK Falstone Old School Tea Rooms, T01434-240459, www.falstonetearoom.co.uk (open from 10.30am Mon–Fri, from 10am at weekends)

PARKING Falstone Old School Tea Rooms car park or at various places in the village

An easy circular walk that takes in part of the forest to the north of Falstone. The route is on waymarked paths and forest tracks. The return section continues through Falstone to visit the sculpture called the Stell on the banks of the River North Tyne.

START From the Tea Rooms turn left onto the road. Walk past the church and under the old railway line to the T-junction. Turn left and then right at the first gate; Falstone Burn is on your left-hand side. To keep away from the muddy section, walk away from the Burn slightly uphill, and as you approach the wood in front of you look for a ladder stile going over the wall and into the wood.

1️⃣ Once over the ladder stile turn right and follow the path through the trees and uphill, with the wall to your right. Keep going on the path, following the waymarkers, which will then direct you left over a small bridge and through a gap in a wall. The route climbs some more, going through the forest and away from the Burn. As you continue the path turns into a wide forest track and makes its way through a clearing to a T-junction, where you turn left.

2️⃣ At the next T-junction on a bend take the left turn into the bend and continue on the track as it comes into a clearing, with views on your left-hand side. Look for the marker post on your left next to a lone tree that indicates a path going left. Take this left turn and follow the path until you reach the T-junction of another forest track, where you turn right. At the next T-junction turn left through a gate and walk down the hill back towards Falstone. Looking right, you can make out the high dam wall of Kielder.

③ Follow the track down to the road, where you turn left then right back under the railway and down the road to the Tea Rooms. Turn left past the Tea Rooms and the United Reformed Church until you come to the River North Tyne, where you turn left. Follow the path alongside the river past the sculpture of the *Stell* and continue until you reach the road bridge, where you turn left. Walk down the field edge to the gate and continue along the path back into Falstone.

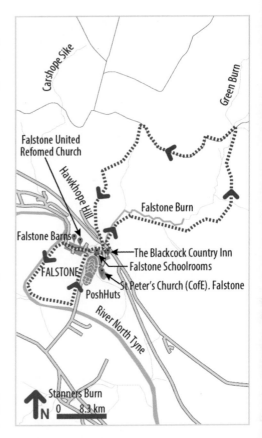

Points of interest

Stell: A stell is an old Norse word that means a stone-walled shelter for sheep, but in this case the artist Colin Wilbourn worked with local people to produce a stone shelter for people. Rectangular in shape, two of the sides are stone three-seater settees complete with stone cushions and steel antimacassars on armrests and settee backs. There is a steel carpet on the floor and access is gained through two gates on the other two sides. Open to the elements, this is a great place to sit and watch the world go by.

Hareshaw Linn

START Centre of Bellingham, GR NY839833

NEAREST POSTCODE NE48 2BA

DISTANCE 3 miles (4.8km)

SUMMARY Easy

MAP OS Explorer OL42 Kielder Water & Forest

WHERE TO EAT AND DRINK There are various pubs and cafés in Bellingham

PARKING In Bellingham village or use the Hareshaw Linn car park at GR NY840834

An easy walk that uses footpaths, steps and footbridges that lead you through the woods close to Hareshaw Burn to visit Hareshaw Linn, a 30ft waterfall.

START From the High St on the B6320, walk down the road signed to West Woodburn and Redesmouth. Cross the bridge over Hareshaw Burn and take the signed footpath on the left immediately after the bridge. Walk past the alternative parking for Hareshaw Linn and continue past the information board about the Hareshaw Ironworks.

1 In damp or wet weather ignore the footpath close to the information board that leads along the Burn, but instead take the track above the footpath. Both routes come out at the same place, which is before a gate that you go through to continue on a track with some paved sections.

2 There are steps and footbridges to negotiate and the track steadily rises until the waterfall is reached. Linn is an old English word for waterfall.

3 The path ends at the waterfall so the route back is just a reverse, with the added enjoyment that it is all more or less downhill.

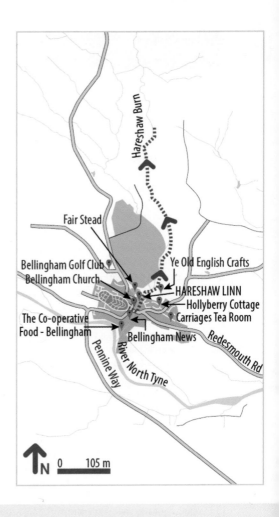

Points of interest

Hareshaw Ironworks: The area around Hareshaw Burn is quite peaceful, but in 1838 this was the site of a large ironworks with blast furnaces, coke ovens, stores and stables in full operation for over 10 years. Delays in getting the railway to Bellingham and mounting transport costs finally forced the the ironworks' closure in 1849.

Walltown to the Milecastle Inn

START The parking area alongside the road, at GR NY674661

NEAREST POSTCODE CA8 7HF

DISTANCE 3 miles (4.8km)

SUMMARY Moderate; this walk can be extended using the Walltown to Once Brewed walk (see below) by continuing along the Wall from Great Chesters, making it 9 miles in total

MAP OS Explorer OL43 Hadrian's Wall

WHERE TO EAT AND DRINK There is a shop at Walltown Quarry Visitor Centre and a café at the Roman Army Museum; The Milecastle Inn, T01434-321372, www.milecastle-inn. co.uk, is on the B6318

A short linear walk that visits some of the best preserved sections of the wall and the Roman fort of Aesica. The walk ends at the Milecastle Inn, where a bus, the AD122, will take you back to Walltown. The bus operates daily between the end of May and the end of August and a timetable can usually be obtained from www.visithadrianswall.co.uk/.

START From the car park walk diagonally uphill to the right to reach Walltown Crags, turn right and follow the path as it descends to cross a stile and and climb the steps to regain the height on the other side of the pass. The path continues along the top, rising and falling as it follows the contours of the ridge line. After passing through a wood, you will pass the farm at Cockmount Hill and beyond you will see the outline of Aesica Roman Fort, whose modern name is Great Chesters.

1 After looking round the site of the fort, cross the ladder stile over the wall and continue to follow the wall line down the field past Burnhead to cross the wall over a stile. Cross the road bridge and turn right on the minor road. Follow this road down and cross the B6318 to arrive at the Milecastle Inn.

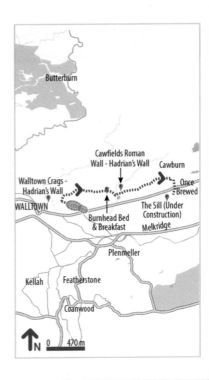

Points of interest

Walltown Visitor Centre is open Apr–end Oct and has a small shop. The toilets are open all year round. Walks led by a National Park Ranger are held over the summer. The car park here has parking charges. Close by and only a short walk away is the Carvoran Roman Army Museum based on the site of Magnis Roman Fort. There is a car park at the museum, which has an entrance fee but is well worth visiting. The museum is open all year except Dec and Jan.

Aesica Roman Fort was built to guard Caw Gap, just over a mile away to the east. In its lifetime the fort was guarded by auxiliary soldiers from modern-day Belgium and Switzerland. The fort was excavated in 1897 and one noticeable feature was the construction of bathhouses fed by aqueducts running for six miles to the north of the wall.

Blanchland & Pennypie

START Blanchland car park (£1 honesty box), GR NY964504

NEAREST POSTCODE DH8 9SS

DISTANCE 3½ miles (5.6km)

SUMMARY Easy

MAP OS Explorer OL43 Hadrian's Wall and OS Explorer 307 Consett & Derwent Reservoir

WHERE TO EAT AND DRINK The White Monk Tearoom, T01434-675044 (open daily 10.30am–5pm); Lord Crewe Arms, www.lordcrewearmsblanchland. co.uk

From Blanchland the path goes along the River Derwent, on the edge of Northumberland and Durham, before heading north along a track across moorland and then returning down an old drovers' road.

START From the car park walk out onto the minor road and turn right. Walk through Blanchland as far as the bridge and take the public footpath indicated through the gap in the wall on the right-hand side. This path will lead you down to the River Derwent and continues alongside the river until it comes out on the road at Baybridge.

[1] Turn right and walk to the crossroads, then straight ahead along the narrow road. The road continues until it curves to the left alongside a wood, where you go through a gate and along a track. Keep on the track with the wall to your right until you cross a bridge at a T-junction. Turn right through a gate with a public footpath sign indicating Blanchland; on your left is Pennypie House. You are now on the Drovers' Road, which took wagons, sheep and cattle up to Hexham. Continue on this track downhill past Shildon and the old mines, where the track becomes a road. Continue on the road until you come to the car park on your right-hand side.

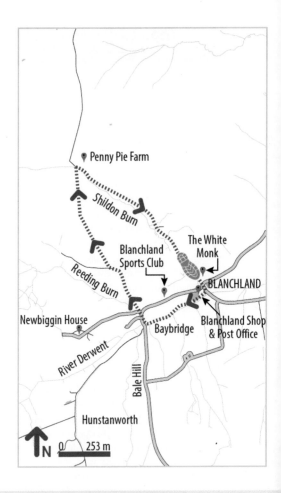

Points of interest

 Pennypie House: So called because it is thought that this was an inn on the drovers' road that sold pies to passers-by for a penny.

Drovers' Road: Going north from Blanchland, the track is an old drovers' road that led across the moors to Hexham. There would also have been traffic along this road from the mines at Shildon.

Druridge Bay & Country Park

START Hadston Scurs car park
(accessed from the minor road off
the A1068), GR NU278007

DISTANCE 3½ miles (5.6km)

SUMMARY Easy

MAP OS Explorer 325 Morpeth &
Blyth

WHERE TO EAT AND DRINK Depending
on the time of year, there is a Visitor
Centre in the Country Park

A nice, easy, short walk along the coast and into the Country Park. The
route goes around the lake and back along the coast. There are activities for
children during the summer months in and around the Visitor Centre.

START From the car park turn left on the track until you reach the
concrete walkway leading down to the beach. Walk onto the beach, turn
right and follow the coastline of Druridge Bay until you reach the second
set of steps on your right. Cross the access road and follow the path into
the Country Park.

① When you reach the edge of the main car park in the park, turn
left and, keeping to the grassed area, follow the road until you meet a
track that is leading right down towards the lake. Follow the path as it
goes to the left around the lake. When you reach the weir you can use
the stepping stones to cross the end of the lake or continue on the path
as it swings around the edge of the lake to cross a footbridge and pass the
stepping stones on the other side.

② Continue around the lake, crossing a concrete footbridge, and just
before the path starts to swing back towards the main car park turn left
on a path that is signed to the beach. This path will lead onto the access
road, where you turn left and then right through a gate that leads across
the field to another gate, where the path goes through the dunes onto the
beach. Turn left and walk back along the beach to the car park.

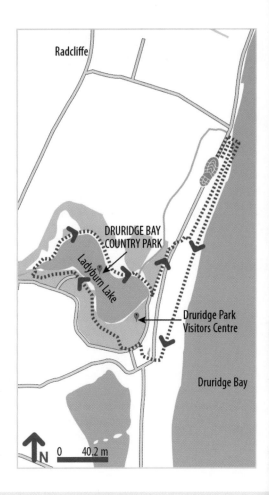

Points of interest

Druridge Bay Country Park: The Visitor Centre has displays and information about the local area, and a café and shop which is open at weekends and during school holidays. The toilets and information area are open daily 9.30am–4.30pm. The café, shop and display rooms are open Apr–Sept 11am–4pm at weekends, on Bank Holidays and during the school summer holidays.

Holystone & Lady's Well

START Holystone Forestry car park, GR NT950025

NEAREST POSTCODE NE65 7AJ

DISTANCE 3½ miles (5.6km)

SUMMARY Easy; a pleasant walk over agricultural land

MAP OS Explorer OL16 The Cheviot Hills

WHERE TO EAT AND DRINK The Cross Keys Inn, Thropton, T01669-620362;The Three Wheat Heads Inn, Thropton, www.threewheatheads.co.uk; there are also more pubs and cafés in Rothbury

Starting from the village of Holystone, the route passes Lady's Well and heads north, crossing the River Coquet at Sharperton. With little effort it gains the high ground above the river before turning back along the wide valley bottom to return to Holystone via a footbridge.

START Walk down the road back towards Holystone village, looking out for a public footpath sign on your left that indicates the way to Holystone across the field. Walk across the field, keeping the house to your right. As you get past the house there is a track leading left towards a group of trees that surrounds Lady's Well. Turn left here and walk to Lady's Well; having visited the well, turn left as you come out of the gate and follow the track round the side of the well to cross a ladder stile with a public footpath marker.

① Continue across the field with the fence line initially to your left, crossing a number of stiles, until you come to a farm track where you turn right, heading towards the buildings at Wood Hall. Turn right on the road and follow it as it bears left across the road bridge and then bends right past the village of Sharperton. Continue on this road until it bears sharp left and go right through a gate with a public footpath sign indicating High Farnham (1 mile).

② Follow the path uphill, with the stream below you to your right, and exit through a gate to cross a field, keeping the bankside to your left. As you gain height you can see the edge of a wood in front of you. Down below and to your right you can see the bridge that you will cross on the way back to Holystone.

③ Go over one stile and then a second to enter the wood, walk through the wood and exit over another stile. Ahead is another wood and in the left-hand corner hiding behind a large tree is another stile to cross. Once across the stile turn right and walk along the field line to the road. Turn right on the road and walk along it a short way until it turns sharp left. On the left there is a public bridleway sign indicating Holystone (1 mile) that is pointing to the right.

④ Turn right through the gate to follow a track down through a wood, crossing a small stream and then exiting the wood through another gate. Follow the track down diagonally left to pass through a metal gate, picking up the marker post that leads you to the footbridge over the River Coquet. Once over the bridge go across the field to exit onto the road, where you turn left. Turn right into Holystone village and follow the road around to the right to pick up the original path that will lead you across the field and over the stile onto the road, where you turn right back to the car park.

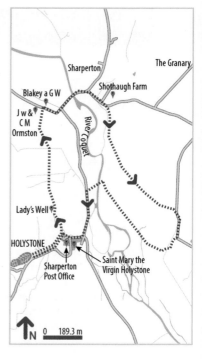

Points of interest

Lady's Well: This is an attractive well, although its shape is a rectangular stone water tank. It has almost certainly changed since St Ninian supposedly came here at Easter 627 to baptise 3,000 people. The statue of St Ninian came here from Alnwick in 1780. It was originally in the well but was replaced with the cross in the nineteenth century.

Kilham Hill Trail

Sᴛᴀʀᴛ Parking area on side of road (grassy lay-by), GR NT881320

Nᴇᴀʀᴇsᴛ ᴘᴏsᴛᴄᴏᴅᴇ TD12 4QS

Dɪsᴛᴀɴᴄᴇ 3½ miles (5.6km)

Sᴜᴍᴍᴀʀʏ Moderate

Mᴀᴘ OS Explorer 339 Kelso, Coldstream & Lower Tweed Valley

Wʜᴇʀᴇ ᴛᴏ ᴇᴀᴛ ᴀɴᴅ ᴅʀɪɴᴋ Cafe Maelmin, Milfield, www. cafemaelmin.co.uk; there are also various cafés and pubs in Wooler

The first section along the old Alnwick to Cornhill railway line gives way to a short but steep climb to the top of Kilham Hill. The views from the top are extensive in all directions, north and west into Scotland, east across farmland to the North Sea and south across the Cheviot hills.

Sᴛᴀʀᴛ From the parking area walk back down the road you have just driven up to the T-junction, cross straight over the road and go through the gate. Cross the field to a metal gate, go through it and turn right onto the old railway line.

1 Walk along the railway line until you reach a fence ahead of you with a stile. Turn right here to follow the path up the hillside through the trees; at the Y-junction keep left and walk through the trees to a ladder stile going over the wall onto the road.

2 Turn left on the road a short distance and go through the first metal gate on your right. Turn diagonally right to walk up the hillside. There is a marker post higher up that you may be able to see to the left of the gorse bushes. Beyond the marker post is a metal gate that you go through. Continue on a visible path as it crests a ridge then descends, before climbing again and swinging right.

3 Go through another metal gate and then left up towards a marker post, where you turn right. As you climb higher there is a marker post to your right, which brings you in line with the cairn at the top of Kilham Hill.

4 From the cairn, follow the path down the hillside, passing some

marker posts until you get to a deer fence. Go through the offset metal gate to continue down the hillside through a new plantation, keeping the fence line to your right.

⑤   At the bottom of the hill go through the metal gate on your right to cross a footbridge over a stream. Climb the bank on the other side, go through the gate at the top and turn right to arrive back at the lay-by.

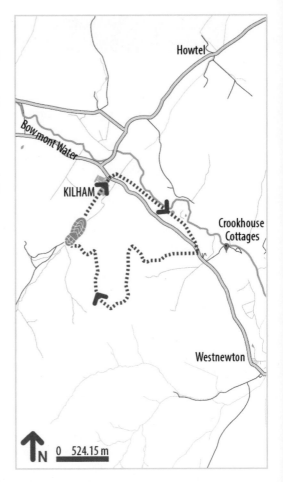

Steel Rigg & Hotbank

START Steel Rigg car park, GR NY750676

NEAREST POSTCODE NE47 7AW

DISTANCE 3½ miles (5.6km)

SUMMARY Hard

MAP OS Explorer OL43 Hadrian's Wall

WHERE TO EAT AND DRINK The Twice Brewed Inn is on the B6318 close to the car park, T01434-344534, www.twicebrewedinn.co.uk

Great views of Hadrian's Wall on the crags above Crag Lough, returning along the line of the wall.

START From the car park go out onto the minor road, turn right and walk along the road to the first public footpath sign on the right. You can see the track going away to your right as you approach the footpath sign. Cross the stile and follow the footpath through several fields, keeping the line of the fence to your left. There are great views of the crags above Crag Lough and further along you can see Hotbank Crags. Another finger-post points the way across an unmarked field.

① As you cross a ladder stile exiting the field system, turn immediately right to cross another ladder stile that will take you down a farm track to Hotbank Farm, which you will pass on your right. Exit from the farm area through a gate and turn right to walk past Milecastle 38 and the main farm track leading into Hotbank Farm.

② As you pass over the farm track there is a choice of paths that you can take. A gate on the right indicates Steel Rigg in 1½ miles. There is a sign to your left pointing to the Roman Military Way, which also indicates Steel Rigg in 1½ miles. The Roman Military Way is a relatively flat track that passes south of the wall, bypassing the climbs and descents that the path along the wall makes. For the most enjoyable section, take the gate to the right, continuing along the wall and eventually crossing it at the famous Sycamore Gap. The final descent is down Peel Crags and then up the grassy slope to follow the path back to the car park.

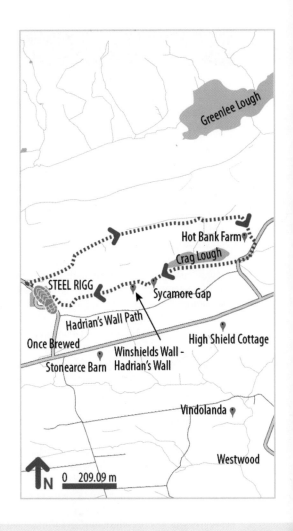

Points of interest

🔍 Sycamore Gap, located east of Steel Rigg, is one of the most photographed images of the whole of Hadrian's Wall. There cannot be many people who have walked this section of the wall and not taken a photograph of this tree.

Vindolanda & Henshaw

Start Vindolanda Visitor Centre car park, GR NY767663

Nearest postcode NE47 7JN

Distance 3½ miles (5.6km)

Summary Easy

Map OS Explorer OL43 Hadrian's Wall

Where to eat and drink There is a small refreshments area at Once Brewed Visitor Centre shop (open April–end Oct); The Twice Brewed Inn, on the B6318, is almost adjacent to the Visitor Centre, T01434-344534, www.twicebrewedinn.co.uk

Starting from the Vindolanda car park, the route goes south down to the attractive village of Henshaw, before turning west then north to return alongside Chainley Burn.

Start Leave the car park and turn left on the minor road, walking down the road until you reach the first track on your left. A finger-post indicates Henshaw (1¼ miles) and Bardon Mill (2 miles); go through the gate and head across the field, passing through a second gate and out onto a track, which you follow, ignoring a track coming in from the left. The track comes out onto a minor road where you turn left; a finger-post indicates Henshaw (½ mile) and Bardon Mill (1¼ miles).

[1] At the Y-junction go straight on past a finger-post indicating Henshaw (¼ mile). At the T-junction turn right; there is an old well on the right-hand corner. Turn left at the first track junction. There is a finger-post hiding in the trees by the stile that indicates Henshaw (¼ mile). Walk down the field edge past Waughs Bank and then turn through a gate to continue down on the other side of the field edge. At the bottom of the field there is a stile to cross, another field and a metal gate leading from a short lane into the small village of Henshaw.

[2] Follow the lane round to your left and turn right at the T-junction; just before the old church there is a gate on the left with a finger-post indicating Parkside (½ mile). Follow the path as it goes slightly uphill, heading towards a telegraph pole. The path crosses several fields, each

with its own gates, and looking right you can see the cars passing on the A69. As you come to a track leading up to Parkside, there is a gate immediately in front of you; go through the gate, turn left and walk up the field line to exit through another gate to the right of the farm. Walk up the farm track and turn right onto a minor road. Where the road bears right there is a gate on the left leading to Cragside Riding Stables, with a finger-post indicating Vindolanda (1 mile) and Hadrian's Wall (1½ miles).

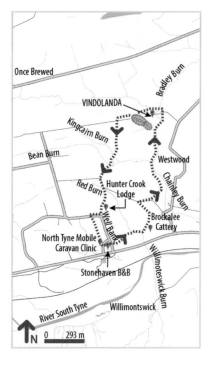

3　Go through the gate and follow the track up and past the riding stables, cross the stream using the footbridge if necessary and continue along the track. Go through several fields using the gates or stiles, and as you crest a rise Vindolanda is in front of you. The path narrows here, with several boardwalk sections and Chainley Burn beginning to appear on your right, and you will come to one of the entrances to Vindolanda Museum and Shop on your left. Walk out of the entrance, turn left and walk down the minor road back into the car park.

Points of interest

Vindolanda Fort, built on the route of the Stangate Road, was one of 13 forts that were staged along the road between Corbridge and Carlisle. Vindolanda was occupied for over 300 years and saw many re-builds as generations of soldiers were stationed here. The Stangate Road provided much of the foundation for the medieval Carelgate or Carlisle Road, but by the mid-eighteenth century it had became unusable by coaches and wagons. The new Military Road, the B6318, was built between 1746 and 1752.

Wooler & Earle Mill

START Burnhouse Rd, Wooler car park, GR NT989281

NEAREST POSTCODE NE71 6BJ

DISTANCE 3½ miles (5.6km)

SUMMARY Easy, level walk that can be done at any time of year

MAP OS Explorer OL16 The Cheviot Hills

WHERE TO EAT AND DRINK There are various cafés and pubs in Wooler

An easy walk out of Wooler, which goes west out of the town and heads south along a path through a valley, giving the impression that you are really out in the countryside.

START From the car park turn right and walk to the T-junction with Wooler High St. Turn right and walk along the High St almost to the end and turn right on Ramsey's La, which is also signed for Wooler Common. Just before the end of the houses on the right, turn left along a track signed for St Cuthbert's Way. At the top of the track go through a gate and follow the public footpath indicating Pin Well (½ mile).

1️⃣ The path leads through a steep-sided valley. As it drops down a slope, there is a solitary tree at the bottom, and to the right of the tree is the Pin Well (GR NT986270). On Ordnance Survey maps the well is marked as a Wishing Well.

2️⃣ Continue on the path, passing through a metal gate, and turn right onto a track that leads down to a minor road. Turn left on the road and at the T-junction turn right. At the next T-junction turn left; there is a public footpath sign indicating Earle Mill (¼ mile) and Wooler (1 mile). At the end of the tarmac track, with Earle Mill on your left, follow the public footpath indicating Wooler (¾ mile). The path goes along the edge of a wood, with a caravan site to the right, until it reaches the road leading up the hill into Wooler. Turn left and walk up the hill onto Wooler High St and back to the car park.

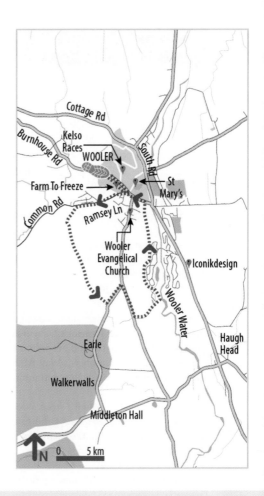

Points of interest

Pin Well: Not much is left of this old well but at one time it was associated with an old story that if you dropped a bent pin into the well and made one special wish it would come true. Unlike other wells which often had a number of coins at the bottom, the Pin Well had various bent pins. As hat pins and hair pins went out of fashion, the name of the well has disappeared.

Housesteads & the Pennine Way

Start Bousesteads Visitor Centre car park, GR NY794684

Nearest postcode NE47 6NN

Distance 3¾ miles (6km)

Summary Hard

Map OS Explorer OL43 Hadrian's Wall

Where to eat and drink The Twice Brewed Inn is on the B6318, nearly 3 miles to the west of Housesteads, To1434-344534, www.twicebrewedinn.co.uk

Starting from Housesteads Information Centre car park, the route goes up to Housesteads Roman Fort, following the path of the Wall to the Pennine Way intersection, and returns north of the Wall with perfect views of Housesteads Crags and the fort situated on top of the crags.

Start From the car park head towards the Information Centre and toilets. In the summer months the access onto the path leading up to Housesteads is through the Information Centre, where you turn right and exit through a door that leads onto the main path just beyond the toilets. In winter, when the Information Centre is closed, go through the arch past the toilets to pick up the same path.

① Go through a gate and walk uphill along the path to the fort, which you pass on the left-hand side. Walk alongside the fort's wall until you meet a gate leading out onto Hadrian's Wall. Turn left and you can walk along the top of the Wall for several hundred yards before coming down some steps and passing through a gate, keeping the Wall on your right. You will go over several ladder stiles as the Wall rises and falls along the crags and at Cuddy's Crags one more ladder stile will bring you to a ladder stile on your right with a finger-post indicating the Pennine Way to the north. Go over this stile and walk down a track, keeping a field wall to your left, until you come to a lime kiln where you turn right along a main track.

② Go over a ladder stile next to the gate, at which point the Pennine Way turns away from you to the left; your route heads towards a group of trees directly in front of you. As you approach the trees go through the gate into the wood, follow the path slightly right and exit through the gate on the other side. You are now heading over the field on an indistinct track, making for the gate that you can see over to the right. The gate, called King's Wicket, cuts through Hadrian's Wall at this point as the wall comes down from the crags at Housesteads.

③ Turn right as you come through the gate and head along the Wall towards Housesteads. As you come through a small wood, go over the stile and at the bottom of the slope head uphill to pass the right-hand side of Housesteads. Pick up the track going downhill back to the Information Centre and car park.

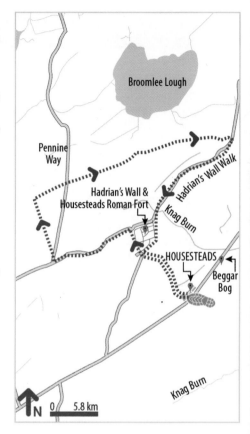

Points of interest

Housesteads Fort was constructed shortly after AD 122, and was occupied for almost 300 years. It was built not long after Hadrian's Wall was finished and could have housed more than 800 auxiliary troops. The fort makes up the most complete example of a Roman fort in Britain.

Sinderhope & the Golf Course

START High Forest Community Centre car park (just off the B6295), Sinderhope, GR NY845520

POSTCODE NE47 9SD (not an active postcode)

DISTANCE 3¾ miles (6km)

SUMMARY Easy. A small hill, a river valley, an old mine and a surprise waterfall near the end – a near perfect walk

MAP OS Explorer OL43 Hadrian's Wall

WHERE TO ET AND DRINK There are various pubs and cafés in Allendale Town, including small speciality shops

A walk uphill to begin with, but then quickly downhill past Allandale Golf Club to walk south along the river. Crossing many footbridges over streams, the route makes its way into old mine workings before re-crossing the river next to an impressive waterfall.

START Leave the car park, turning left along the B6295, and continue along the road until just after the bridge, where the road bends to the left. On the right-hand side there is a public footpath indicating East Garret's Hill (¼ mile). Follow the footpath up the hill, aiming for a stile that is to the left of the house. Cross the stile, pass through a small wood and over a wall stile, continuing up the hill and keeping to the right, until you turn right between two walls to pass through a gate onto a minor road.

① Turn left and continue along the road, passing the left turn to High Studdon, and then turn left at the next minor road, which leads downhill past Allendale Golf Club. This road drops down to a T-junction with the B6295. Cross the road and go through the left-hand gate to head downhill on a zigzag track to cross a bridge at the bottom over the River East Allen. Turn left over the stile and follow the path beside the river, going through the farm at Parks. There are a number of stiles, gates and footbridges to negotiate along this stretch of the route.

② The path gradually climbs a rise, moves away from the river and reaches a four-way finger-post. Straight ahead is Pry Hill, to the right is Crowberry and to your rear is signed Parks. Take the left-hand indicator to Holms Linn, going downhill and back towards the river. This is a neglected section of the route; most of the walk boards are broken and dangerous and, depending on the time of year, the whole area is muddy underfoot. It is a relatively short section, which ends as you go over a stile leading out of the woods.

③ Walk past the mine workings of Holms Linn and cross the footbridge over the river close to a fine waterfall. Turn right and follow the path as it climbs up to the stile at the minor road. Cross the road and over another stile that is signed to the Community Centre.

④ Walk up the slope, keeping close to the stream running downhill, and look for a stile on the right, which is in the bend of the fence line on the far side of the stream. Cross the stile, turn left over another stile and walk up the field to enter the rear yard of the Community Centre.

Points of interest

The mine workings of Holms Linn form part of the Blackett Level, a tunnel that was intended to run from Allendale to Allenheads. Because of the collapse of the lead mining industry in 1903, only 4½ miles of the planned 7 miles were completed. The shaft here dropped about 330ft into the tunnel. There were four shafts: two are further up the valley towards Allenheads at Sipton and Breckonholme and the other is closer to Allendale at Studdondene.

13 | West Hill & St Gregory's Hill

Start Car parking area next to
Kirknewton Activity Centre,
GR NT914302

Nearest postcode NE71 6XG

Distance 3¾ miles (6km)

Summary Moderate

Map OS Explorer OL16 The Cheviot
Hills

Where to eat and drink Cafe
Maelmin, Milfield,
www.cafemaelmin.co.uk;
there are also various cafés and
pubs in Wooler

A short walk from the village of Kirknewton to the top of two small hill forts
on the edge of the Cheviots. St Gregory's Hill is named after the church in
Kirknewton.

Start From the parking area walk past the church, which is on your
right, turn left at the T-junction and then right on a tarmac lane that
leads you away from the village. The tarmac gives way to a rough track
that swings slowly left around West Hill.

1 Ignore the permissive path sign on your right and continue on the
rough track as it continues round the hillside. Go through a metal gate
next to a small wood on your right and another gate at the end of the
wood, before turning left up the hillside.

2 Go past the old stone ruins to reach a gate with a ladder stile. Go
over the stile and bear diagonally left, heading towards a fence line. Go
over the stile at the fence line and continue up the hill to reach the cairn
and hill fort on top of West Hill.

3 Return to the stile, go over it and keep to the left to cross the
open ground in front of you. You will reach a wall stile, which you
cross, and then continue over some old stepping stones by a stream.
Head towards the wall that you can see ahead but begin to swing
left to head uphill, passing a marker post. Continue to the top of
St Gregory's Hill and the hill fort, with a good view down into
Kirknewton.

④ Retrace your path down the hill to approach the wall on your right; in the bottom corner there is gate which you go through to pick up a clear path swinging left down the hillside. Continue on the path as it swings left parallel with the road below and you will see a wall stile next to a gate. Go over the wall stile and turn left, following the minor road leading into the rear of Kirknewton, and turn right to pass the church and reach the car park.

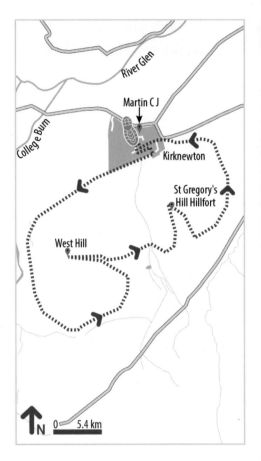

Points of interest

St Gregory's Church: A church is recorded here in the twelfth century but there could have been a church on this site or close to it from earlier times. Ad-Gefrin, an early Anglo Saxon royal residence, lies a mile away from Kirknewton, and Paulinus, sent to England by Pope Gregory in AD 601, was at Ad-Gefrin preaching and converting around the year AD 627. A great treasure of the church is a twelfth-century stone carving depicting the Adoration of the Magi.

Allendale Town & The Hope

Start Allendale Town main square, GR NY838558

Postcode NE47 9BJ

Distance 4 miles (6.4km)

Summary Moderate, over mixed terrain

Map OS Explorer OL43 Hadrian's Wall

Where to eat and drink There are various pubs and cafés in Allendale Town, including small speciality shops

A moderate walk with great views down into the Allendale valley at the highest point. This walk can be combined with the Allendale Town and River East Allen walk (see below), making an 8½-mile loop.

Start Keep to the right of the town square and head downhill on the road that leads past the Allendale Inn. As the road bears left, take the track on the right signposted Allendale Bridge. This will lead down to the footpath next to the River East Allen. On this section of the walk you will pass a tunnel called the Blackett Level.

1 Continue along the footpath until you reach the remains of a bridge; there is metal fencing overlooking the river at this point. On the right are two gates; go through the left-hand gate and follow the remains of the old railway line to exit through a gate onto the B6295. A short distance on the right go through another gate and follow the tree line on the left to exit over a low wall onto the B6303.

2 Go straight across the road and follow the footpath to the left of the house, steadily climbing the hillside with a wall to your left. Just before the building of Housty go diagonally right through a gate and then over a wall stile. Continue along the path at first with the wall to your right, crossing several stiles and with the wall line changing to your left-hand side, until you reach the covered reservoir which is to your left. Continue on, heading downhill to cross a stile and turning right down an enclosed track to exit onto the minor road called Leadside Bank.

3 Turn left and walk up the road, before turning right across a cattle grid onto a farm track. Continue across several fields until you come to the ruined farm of Moor House. Although it is possible to walk on the track past the ruins, it can be extremely muddy. It is better to take the path round the rear of the house and to cross a small stile on the far side of the ruin. From here, head across the farm track, heading downhill away from the ruin to cross a wall stile and then a footbridge.

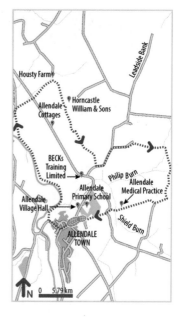

4 Once over the footbridge follow the path down and through the farm buildings of Bull's Hill and then, on the track leading away from the farm, turn right to head towards the building at Portgate. Turn right once past the first building, then turn left past the house and through the gate in front of you. Go straight ahead across the field, through a gate and, just before the wood, turn left through another gate and then immediately right. The path heads downhill across a footbridge and then there's a short uphill section that comes out on the minor road above the town. Head downhill on Shilburn Rd past the Fire Station and school, turning left at the bottom of the road to get back to the main square. On the way back to the square you will pass a memorial fountain to John Joseph Glendenning, who was killed on 7 March 1902 during the Boer War.

Points of interest

As you walk along the riverside on the first part of the walk, you will pass the entrance to the Blackett Tunnel. This was an ambitious project that was designed to drive a tunnel 7 miles from Allendale to Allenhead. The object was to find new veins of lead in the valley and to draw water from the mines at Allenhead. The project was started on 4 October 1855 but in 1896, with only 4½ miles of tunnel complete, the tunnel was abandoned, although work continued within the completed section until 1903.

Alnmouth, Lesbury & the Coast

Start Beach car park, Alnmouth, GR NU250106

Distance 4 miles (6.4km)

Summary Easy

Map OS Explorer 332 Alnwick & Amble

Where to eat and drink There are various pubs and cafés in Alnmouth

Starting at the estuary with the River Aln, the walk follows the river to Lesbury, then climbs a small hill to drop down through a golf course onto the beach back into Alnmouth.

Start The route starts from the car park on the beach, from where you head towards the town at the end of the car park, initially taking the path that leads to the shops and cafés. Bear left after the information board to walk over the dunes and, providing the tide is out, onto the river estuary of the River Aln. You can follow the estuary round and come up the steps beside the old Ferry Hut onto the road. If the tide is in, just follow the road close to the estuary wall until you arrive at the Ferry Hut. From here, continue along the road, turning left at the footpath just before the road curves right back into the town.

1 The footpath is at the back of the children's playground and called Lovers Walk. Follow the path until it comes out at the bridge on the B1338; cross the road and turn left over the pedestrian bridge. As you walk along the road you will pick up a footpath on the right, which will bring you to a gate. On the opposite side of the gate is a small car park and the remains of a gate and sign to Lesbury that points up the field edge. Walk up the field edge to the left of a cricket pitch in the direction of Lesbury. At the end of the field edge turn right through a gate past the rear of the houses to cross a bridge over the river.

2 Turn sharp right after crossing the bridge and head for another smaller footbridge that crosses a stream close to the river. A sign points the way to both Alnmouth and Foxton Hall in 1¼ miles. Follow the path, keeping close to the river, but as the river bends to the right take the higher of the two paths that divide here, heading uphill. After passing

through the cultivated field, go through a gate and angle left up towards a telegraph pole at the top of the field. Go over the stile and take the road directly opposite leading to Alnmouth Golf Club and Foxton Hall.

③ When you reach the clubhouse turn diagonally right under the trees to head over part of the course to reach a path that leads down to a main path. The main signed footpath continues straight on past a small group of caravans, but instead turn left and head down the path, crossing a small area of the golf course, to arrive on the sand dunes. From here you can either walk along the sand dunes path back to the car park or walk on the wide expanse of beach.

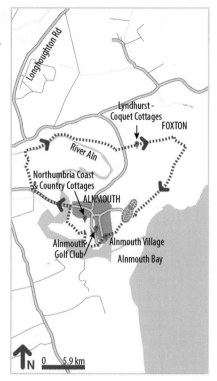

Points of interest

Alnmouth was once an important grain port supplying the growing industrial towns to the south. Even the storm of 1806 that altered the course of the river, separating the town from Church Hill, did little to alter the trade. But by the 1800s ships were being built of iron and steel, which could be damaged by mooring in the small harbour of Alnmouth. As the railway network was developed, the grain export declined completely, replaced by day visitors coming in via the railway and after World War I by motor car.

Probably the smallest museum in the country, the old Ferry Hut provides further information about Alnmouth. The Ferry Hut was used until 1966 by ferrymen rowing passengers across the River Aln.

Biddlestone & Singmoor

Start Parking area in Biddlestone,
GR NT960083

Postcode NE65 7DT

Distance 4 miles (6.4km)

Summary Easy

Map OS Explorer OL16 The Cheviot
Hills

Where to eat and drink Rose
and Thistle, Alwinton, www.
roseandthistlealwinton.com;
Clennell Hall Country House,
Clennell,
www.clennellhallcountryhouse.com

This is a nice uphill walk, generally following a farm track past the buildings of Singmoor and providing an introduction to the varied countryside on this edge of the Cheviots.

Start From the parking area head uphill and go past Harden Quarry on the left. Continue up the track, which will bend to the right before heading further up the hill. There are several gates to go through, but after the last one the track will continue towards the house at Singmoor.

1 Walk past the house through a gate and continue on a path past a wood on your right. You will see a marker post on the skyline and the path continues ahead. After passing another marker post and coming close to the fence line on your left, you will meet another marker post that indicates a bridleway straight ahead and a public footpath to the right. Turn right almost immediately behind you and follow the footpath across the field.

2 There are occasional marker posts, but you are heading towards the wood in front of you. As you approach the wood you will see a gate just to the right of the wood and a stile to the right of the gate. Do not go over the fence, but instead turn diagonally right to follow a path across the field. The path is heading towards the farm track that you can see ahead of you. As you approach the farm track, you will cross a stream and then a gate that you came to when walking up to Singmoor. Go through the gate and walk back down the track to the parking area.

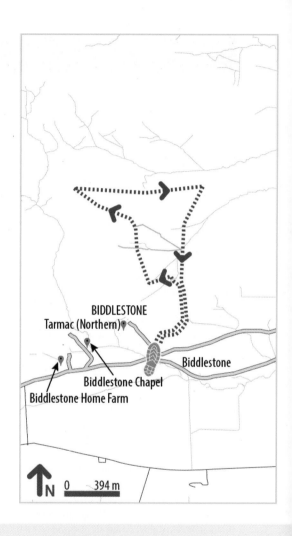

BIDDLESTONE

Tarmac (Northern)

Biddlestone

Biddlestone Chapel

Biddlestone Home Farm

N   0   394 m

Points of interest

Harden Quarry: The quarry has been operating since the 1930s and produces a distinct red stone known as Harden Red, which is often used for demarcation and decorative applications. The courtyards of Buckingham Place and the Mall in London are paved with this product.

Cawfields & Hallpeat Moss

START Cawfields Quarry car park,
GR NY712665

NEAREST POSTCODE NE49 9NN

DISTANCE 4 miles (6.4km)

SUMMARY Moderate; a scenic walk
that takes in an area to the south of
Hadrian's Wall

MAP OS Explorer OL43 Hadrian's
Wall

WHERE TO EAT AND DRINK There is a
shop at Cawfields Quarry (seasonal,
but toilets open all year round);
The Milecastle Inn, T01434-321372,
www.milecastle-inn.co.uk, is on the
B6318

Starting from the car park in Cawfields Quarry, the route heads south over
the Vallum and passes the hidden remains of several Roman camps and forts
to cross the B6318 and pick up a track that has great views of the line of the
Wall to the north. The route re-crosses the B6318 to pick up the Wall along
Cawfield Crags back to the car park.

START From the car park turn left onto the minor road, and as the
road curves there is a public footpath sign on your left indicating
Caw Gap (1 mile). Go through the gate and follow the footpath as it
passes to the left of Cawfield Quarry. As you approach the end of the
fence line on your left, turn right and follow a path down to rejoin the
minor road. Cross the B6318 and take the minor road opposite. The
Milecastle Inn is on your left. On the first curve of this minor road
go left over a ladder stile; the public footpath sign indicates Hallpeat
Moss (1 mile).

1   After going over the stile, go diagonally left to pick up a path
that keeps fairly close to a wall line on your left. The path will start
to go diagonally right on a narrower path, heading towards a small
ridge that is to your right. Cross a ladder stile below the ridge line
and continue alongside a wall until you come out onto a minor road
through a metal gate, where you turn left and walk down to the
B6318, passing a caravan site on your right and Hallpeat Moss Farm
on your left.

②   Cross the B6318 to pick up a footpath on the other side of the road. Follow the path down to the end of the fence and wall line and turn diagonally left to cross the Vallum on a footbridge. Continue on the path up an incline, ignoring a ladder stile to your left. Go through the next gate on your left, cross the minor road and go through the gate opposite signed to Cawfields Quarry (1 mile). Continue along the Wall and after leaving Milecastle 42 turn left in the dip, go through a gate and follow the footpath back to the car park.

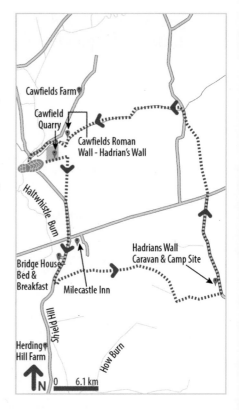

Points of interest

Cawfields Quarry was opened up in 1902 and a single-track tramway was built to take crushed stone down to the loading docks at Haltwhistle to the south. In 1929 the central section of the Wall was sold off and, while the National Trust bought part of the land, it did not own the mineral rights. Consequently the quarry was able to expand and started to demolish the section of Wall above the quarry face. Because of a public outcry the government was forced to act and by compensating the quarry company the demolition ceased. All work at the quarry finished in 1952. If you walk up the steps close to Milecastle 42 while on this route, you will get to the place where the Wall was chopped off by the quarry.

Cottingwood Common Circular

START Leisure Centre car park, Morpeth, GR NZ198857

POSTCOCDE NE61 1PR

DISTANCE 4 miles (6.4km)

SUMMARY Easy; country and riverside paths, and Carlisle Park in Morpeth

MAP OS Explorer 325 Morpeth & Blyth

WHERE TO EAT AND DRINK There are various pubs and cafés in Morpeth

PARKING Morpeth operates a free car park scheme with a 3-hour parking period, apart from Staithes Lane Long Stay car park, which is all day. The scheme uses parking disks, which can be purchased locally

A walk around the northern edge of Morpeth on country paths and in some ancient woodland. Although perhaps better in spring or summer to see the plants and flowers at their best, this is still a good walk to do at any time.

START From the Leisure Centre walk to the Market Pl and cross the road by the mini-roundabout. Head straight up Newgate St until you reach the church of St James the Great and turn right through the stone arch. Pass to the left of the church onto the road and left again onto Cottingwood La.

1 Walk to the end of the lane past the school entrance and take the path that leads straight on past the school playing fields, where a public footpath sign indicates Cottingwood Common. Just before going down the steps, turn right to pick up a path that leads through the wooded area. Go through the gate and bear left on a wide curving field; this was part of the old racecourse. Follow the curve, going through several gates, until you come to a stile. Go over the stile and to the left is a gate, which you go through; follow the path across open land.

2 Go through another gate and you are on the edge of the hospital grounds for a short way before passing through another gate and into

Bluebell Wood. Walk through the wood, following the path as it swings to the right. Close to the road there is an information board and a three-way public footpath indicator. The indicator to the left shows the way to Bothal along a riverside path, but ignore this and go straight on towards Morpeth.

3 The path ends at a flight of steps leading down to a lay-by beside the road. Cross the road at the crossing point and go right down a lane beside the river. The lane leads past a supermarket and the entrance to Staithes Lane car park and ends on the road leading into Morpeth town centre. Follow the road as it swings left past the mini-roundabout and then left at St George's Church to cross Telford Bridge.

4 Cross the road at the pelican crossing, turn left and walk the short distance to enter Carlisle Park. To walk back to the Leisure Centre turn right after passing the aviary on your right and follow the path until it reaches the river. Turn left and walk along the riverside until you cross the footbridge back into the Leisure Centre car park.

Points of interest

Carlisle Park: This park was gifted to Morpeth by the Countess of Carlisle in 1916 and in summer it has an abundance of colourful flowerbeds. It also contains the remains of two castles: the motte and bailey of an eleventh-century castle and the gatehouse of a later castle built in the fourteenth century. Both can be reached with a little climbing from within the park.

Morpeth Racecourse: This was built around 1730, although races were held before then. It was a popular if small venue for over 100 years, with the last race meeting taking place on 10 May 1883.

Harbottle & Drake's Stone

START Harbottle Forestry car park, GR NT926048

MAP OS Explorer OL16 The Cheviot Hills

NEAREST POSTCODE NE65 7BB

DISTANCE 4 miles (6.4km)

SUMMARY Moderate

WHERE TO EAT AND DRINK The Star Inn, Harbottle, T01669-650221;
The Rose and Thistle, Alwinton, www.roseandthistlealwinton.com;
The Three Wheat Heads Inn, Thropton, www.threewheatheads. co.uk

From the car park the route leads uphill towards Drake's Stone and Harbottle Lake. It then drops down through a pleasant forest across the River Coquet and returns via road and track on the north side of Harbottle.

START Leave the Forestry car park by climbing the track that leads up the hill; there is a sign in the car park pointing the way to Drake's Stone. Walk to the edge of the wood and turn right after passing through a gate. Continue uphill with the wood line on your right; as you climb higher you can see the Drake Stone on your left. There are several paths on the left leading to it through the heather – turn left on one of them to climb right up to the stone.

1 On leaving the stone, head towards the path that leads close beside Harbottle Lake and continue alongside the lake until you reach a stile, where you turn right to follow a path uphill through the heather. At the top of the small rise is a wood and directly in front and leading through the wood there is a path which you follow.

2 Continue all the way through the wood until you exit through a gate and turn right on a track leading downhill to the road. Turn left on the road, cross the road bridge over the River Coquet and continue until you reach a public bridleway sign on the right indicating Park House (½ mile) and Harbottle (1¼ miles). Turn right here and follow the minor road uphill towards Park House, passing Low Alwinton Lime Kiln on the left. After Park House the road becomes a track, but continue

onwards with good views of Drake's Stone on your right and Harbottle Castle coming into view ahead.

③ The track goes downhill and takes a right-hand bend, leading you close to the river. As you walk along this section, look out for the footbridge on your right that will lead you back across the river. Follow the path around to the right to join a minor road that leads to the road through Harbottle. Continue through the village, passing Harbottle Castle on your right (worth a visit), and back to the Forestry car park.

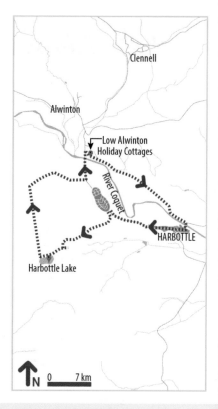

Points of interest

Drake's Stone: This large boulder stone some 30ft high was said (in mostly Victorian literature) to have healing powers, especially if you passed children around it.

Harbottle Castle: Built at Henry II's request in 1160 by the Umfraville family, this now ruined castle has a long history. It has a connection with the union of England and Scotland when in 1515 Margaret Tudor gave birth to a daughter also called Margaret within the castle. The young Margaret had a son, Henry Stuart, who was to become the second husband of Mary, Queen of Scots and together they had a son who was to become James VI of Scotland and James I of England after the death of Elizabeth I.

Hartside & Linhope Spout

Start Grass verge at Hartside, GR NT976162

Nearest postcode NE66 4LY

Distance 4 miles (6.4km)

Summary Easy

Map OS Explorer OL16 The Cheviot Hills

Where to eat and drink Plough Inn, Powburn, T01665-578769; Queens Head, Glanton, T01665-578324; Poachers Rest, Hedgeley Services, T01665-578664

An easy walk on tracks and paths leading to Linhope Spout, the highest straight-drop waterfall in the Cheviots (60ft). The return route has some great views of the hills to the south. The minor road starts from Ingram and has some good places to stop alongside the River Breamish.

Start Walk down the minor road past Hartside and after crossing the bridge over Linhope Burn turn left and then right. Go through a gate and follow the track steadily uphill, keeping the wood line to your right. As you get to the edge of the wood there is a sign on your right with a path leading off to Linhope Spout; ignore this and continue along the main track.

1 Go through a gate and then downhill on the track towards another gate. Do not go through this gate but instead turn right and follow the footpath around to the right of the sheep fold, and then follow Linhope Burn as it flows downstream. This path will take you to the top of Linhope Spout, where you can look over the top as it plunges into the pool at the bottom.

2 Climb down the rocky path to the right of the waterfall and then out to the grassy area beyond. To return back to Hartside you can take the path going diagonally uphill or continue along the burn until you reach a fence line and then follow this uphill. Both these routes will bring you back to the edge of the wood, where you return back to Hartside.

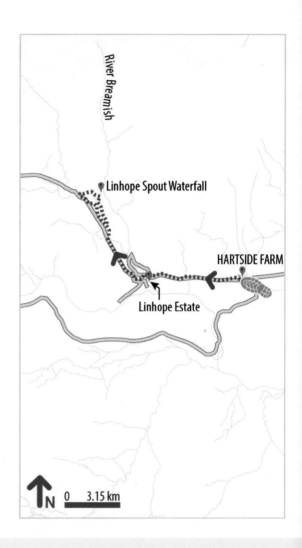

Points of interest

Linhope Spout is a 6oft (18m) chute of water, which lands in a plunge pool 6ft wide and 16ft deep.

Holystone & Dove Crag

START Holystone Forestry car park,
GR NT950025

NEAREST POSTCODE NE65 7AJ

DISTANCE 4 miles (6.4km)

SUMMARY Easy

MAP OS Explorer OL16 The Cheviot
Hills

WHERE TO EAT AND DRINK The Cross
Keys Inn, Thropton, T01669-620362;
The Three Wheat Heads Inn,
Thropton, www.threewheatheads.
co.uk; there are also more pubs and
cafés in Rothbury

A walk that follows a minor road at first, before entering a wooded area
that leads to a hidden crag with a waterfall. The return is mostly through
woodland, but there are good views north into the Cheviots.

START Leave the car park and turn right on the minor road. Keep on the
road until you come to a restricted byway sign on your left that indicates
a right turn to Rockey's Hall (1¾ miles). Turn right and head into the
tree line. The path comes out on a track, where you turn right.

1 As you start down the track you will come to a restricted byway
marker post on your right and a small cleared area on the left. Going
left into the trees at this point is a path, which you follow. The path
will widen out and swing left before climbing a rise and coming to a
T-junction.

2 In front of you there is a marker post and a path that seems to
disappear into the trees. Follow the path through the trees and you will
come to a stream. On the left are the rocks of Dove Crag and you need to
follow the stream until you arrive at the waterfall.

3 When you leave the waterfall, head to your left and you will rejoin
the original path; if you look to your right you will see the marker post.
Turn left and as you follow the path it will come to what looks like a
Y-junction; bear left here and the path will start to go through the trees
until you come out on a broad track. Turn left on the track and continue
until the track starts to swing left. On the right there is a marker post

where you turn right, passing an old bench on your left-hand side.

(4) Just after the bench turn right on a fairly wide path with a moss-covered wall on your right. Continue along this path, passing through an open area, and the path will start to go downhill through a much older wood. There is a fence line to your left, but as you go down the hill begin to move to your right, skirting another fence line on your right. You will come to a clearing, where you bear right to follow a clear path with a bank on your left.

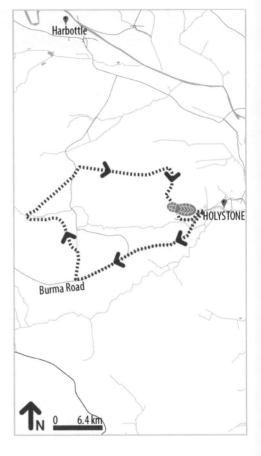

(5) As you walk this section of path, look for a stile over the bank to your left. Go over the stile and continue downhill, passing through several gates until you come to the farm track leading back up to Campville. Turn left and follow the track down to the minor road, where you turn left and walk into the car park.

Walltown & Thirlwall Castle

START Parking area alongside the road, GR NY674661

NEAREST POSTCODE CA8 7HF

DISTANCE 4 miles (6.4km)

SUMMARY Moderate; this walk can be extended using the Walltown and the Vallum walk (Walk 34) to create a loop of 8½ miles

MAP OS Explorer OL43 Hadrian's Wall

WHERE TO EAT AND DRINK There is a shop at Walltown Quarry Visitor Centre and a café at the Roman Army Museum

Starting from the parking area close to Walltown Quarry Visitor Centre, the walk includes a section of the Wall before heading into Walltown Quarry and then in scenic countryside north of the Wall. There are good views of Walltown Crags on the return part of the walk, which includes a visit to Thirlwall Castle.

START From the parking area walk uphill to reach the western end of Walltown Crags, and turn left to follow one of the best preserved sections of the Roman Wall. The Wall comes to an end overlooking Walltown Quarry. Turn left and follow the path down the hillside to pass through a gate on the right and continue the descent into the quarry. Keep on the main path; at the Y-junction bear right and at the next Y-junction bear left to arrive at Walltown Quarry Visitor Centre.

1 Cross the car park and exit through a gate signed to the Labyrinth. The path will come to a T-junction; bear right to visit the Labyrinth but look left and you will see a wooden gate that you will exit through on the return from the Labyrinth. When you exit the gate, turn right and walk along the grassy track to the left of the minor road. At the junction take the left-hand track signed to Low Old Shields (¼ mile). The track curves down past the farm and goes through a gate between the farm and the farm buildings. At the rear of the farm go through a wooden gate on your left and turn right, keep left of the wall, and follow it down the field. At you approach the ladder stile on your right begin to angle left, passing

a marker sign that indicates the route. Closer to the road there is a stile on your left that leads to a footbridge and stepping stones over Tipalt Burn.

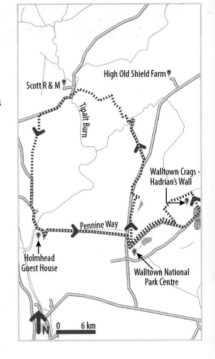

② Turn left on the road; if you would like to do a shorter walk there is a gate through a wall on your left that leads to the Tipalt Burn walk (Walk 55), which will bring you out below Thirlwall Castle. Continuing on the main walk, just before the cattle grid turn left over the wall stile; looking across the field you will see a second stile that you need to head for. There follows a third and then a final stile that will lead onto a downhill section of road that takes you to Thirlwall Castle.

③ After visiting the castle continue down the track, crossing a footbridge over the burn and then heading on the winding path uphill. If you have followed the Tipalt Burn walk and want to visit the castle, turn right over the footbridge and then return on the same path. The path gradually levels out, goes over a ladder stile and exits onto the road through a gate. Go directly across the road onto a track, turning right at the first junction to return to Walltown Quarry Visitor Centre. A short return walk will bring you back to the car park.

Points of interest

Thirlwall Castle is more of a stronghold than a castle. It was built in the twelfth century and later fortified with stones taken from the Roman Wall. It was the home of the Thirlwall family until 1738, when by the marriage of Eleanor Thirlwall to Matthew Swinburne the estate was sold in 1748 and was never occupied thereafter.

Allendale Town & the River East Allen

START Allendale Town main square, GR NY838558

POSTCODE NE47 9BJ

DISTANCE 4½ miles (7.24km)

SUMMARY Moderate

MAP OS Explorer OL43 Hadrian's Wall

WHERE TO EAT AND DRINK There are various pubs and cafés in Allendale Town, including small speciality shops

This walk climbs out of Allendale to the east and stays on high ground before crossing the River East Allen and making the return journey mostly along the Allen Valley, following the route of Isaac's Tea Trail. The walk can be combined with the Allendale Town and The Hope walk (see above), making an 8½-mile loop.

START From the main square walk across the B6303 and a short distance to the left of the telephone box there is a well set into the wall. This is Isaac's Well. Go up the short flight of steps beside the well and follow a path through the housing estate. The path leads out into a field and goes diagonally right to go over a wall stile. Continue up the hill, crossing several fields and stiles, before crossing over the private road.

① Follow the path across more fields as it starts to bear left towards High Scotch Hall. Cross over a wall stile and head towards the barn at the end of the field. Cross a final wall stile to exit onto the farm track, where you turn right and continue along the track until you turn right at the T-junction on the minor road. Walk along the road until you come to the Low Parkgates, where you turn right to follow the path down through the woods.

② The path through the woods comes out on the B6295, where you turn left and continue along the road until you come to the crossroads with the road to Allendale Golf Club on your left. Turn right here and go through the gate in front of you, ignoring the track that leads into the farm. The track zigzags down the hill to cross the River East Allen over a bridge.

③ Turn right after the bridge and follow the path, keeping the river on your right. You are now following Isaac's Tea Trail on its way back to Allendale. A short distance along this track it starts to move away from the river and passes a small cottage, before making its way up a slope and through a gate. Just after the gate look for a marker post on the high ground to your right and follow this up onto the high ground. The track makes its way across several fields, slowly heading right back towards the river. The track comes out on the road beside the bridge, where you turn right and head uphill into Allendale.

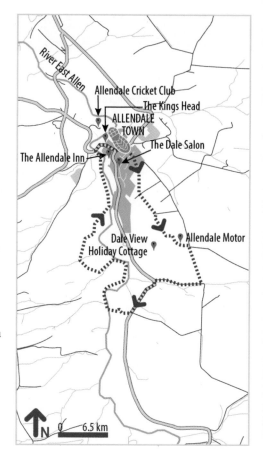

Points of interest

Isaac's Well is named after Isaac Holden, who raised the funds for its construction in 1849. It used to be on the opposite side of the road, but was moved to its present position in 1870 when a piped water supply was installed. Isaac Holden funded other projects for the community in the Allendale Valley and is buried in St Cuthbert's Church in Allendale. Isaac's Tea Trail starts and finishes from the well.

Berthele's Stone & Hepburn Wood

Start Hepburn Woods car park, GR
NU071247

Nearest postcode NE66 4EG

Distance 4½ miles (7.2km)

Summary Moderate

Map OS Explorer 332 Alnwick &
Amble

Where to eat and drink The
Tankerville Arms, Eglingham,
www.tankervillearms.com

The route goes through Hepburn Woods, with an optional climb up to
Berthele's Stone. The return includes a slow ascent to the crags above the
wood, with an easy return along a heather-covered path and through an Iron
Age hill fort.

Start From the car park take the track into the wood past the metal
barrier. At the Y-junction bear left; over to the right at the Y-junction
is a Bronze Age burial site. Just after the Y-junction on the left-hand
side is a gap in the trees, with a faint path leading up the hillside to
Berthele's Stone. There used to be a marker at this point but perhaps
because of the tree-felling, some natural and some man-made, the
marker has gone and the path is difficult to follow. However, the path
leads up and over an old forest track and just above is the large boulder
called Berthele's Stone. There used to be a path that led around the
stone and down to re-emerge on the original track, but it is easiest if
you return by the same route.

1 Once back on the original track continue in the same direction,
keeping right at the next Y-junction. As the track descends through
the wood it becomes more of a dirt track and makes a turn to the right,
with an open field to the left. Just before the open field is a bridge over
a stream with an indistinct path going left just before the bridge. The
path crosses the stream and turns left at a fence line to reach a fence
corner turning right. Follow the fence as it turns right and then go
through the gate on your right-hand side.

2 Follow the path left along the edge of the wood and then left to

a gate with a public bridleway sign. Go through the gate and then diagonally right uphill across the field, heading towards a gate. Go through the gate and continue uphill to the next gate straight ahead. After the second gate continue uphill to reach a wall with a gate. Go through the gate and turn left to follow the path uphill to the crags, with a wall and then a fence line to your left.

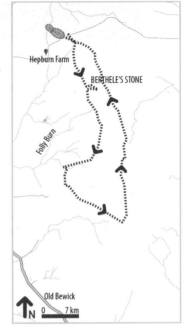

3   When you reach the broken fence line in front of you, you can cross it or turn right to reach an opening in the fence; the gate is also broken. Whether you have crossed the fence or gone through the opening, the path stays fairly close to the fence line on your left, over which the ground drops steeply into Hepburn Wood. There are quite a few paths through the heather and bracken, some of which are tempting but lead you away to the right. As you continue along the path the trees to your left begin to thin out and the path approaches the hill fort on the edge of Hepburn Crags. Follow the path through the hill fort and then down between the large boulders to reach a ladder stile. Go over the ladder stile and continue down to the track, where you turn right back to the car park.

Points of interest

Berthele's Stone: This is a large stone boulder that has dropped from the crags, which lie behind it further into the woods. It has an unusual name but in reality is named after Felix Berthele, a German World War II POW who stayed in England after the war and became a forestry worker. He would follow the forestry ploughs as they laid the many woods that cover the hillsides of Northumberland and collect and record the finds of flints, stone tools and the occasional cup-marked stone. His excellent collection of finds is now displayed at Chillingham Castle.

Carey Barn & Broadstruther

START Car parking area north of the Carey Burn Bridge, GR NT975249

NEAREST POSTCODE NE71 6RE

DISTANCE 4½ miles (7.2km)

SUMMARY Easy

MAP OS Explorer OL16 The Cheviot Hills

WHERE TO EAT AND DRINK There are various cafés and pubs in Wooler

After an easy walk along the Carey Burn valley, the route bears left and climbs out of the valley before a longer uphill section after leaving Broadstruther. The walk returns high above the Carey Burn, before coming slowly downhill back to the parking area. This walk can be combined with the Happy Valley and North Middleton walk (see below) to create a 9-mile loop.

START Walk towards the Carey Burn Bridge and just before it on the right-hand side cross a stile to follow the path that begins beside the burn. This path follows the line of the burn but often moves some distance away from it and then quite high above it as it follows the line of the valley.

[1] At the end of the valley the path rejoins the burn and swings left to join the main track coming down from Wooler Common. Follow this track along the valley bottom with the burn on your left until you come to a bridge, which you cross, and then turn right to follow the path up the slope. Once clear of a small group of trees, the path continues with the burn in the valley to your left until you come to a gate. Go through the gate and you will come to some marker posts. Ignore the one pointing right but continue straight on to cross a small bridge over Broadstruther Burn. The main track to Broadstruther is to your right but ignore this and go straight ahead toward the stone sheep pens and the bridge over Hazelly Burn.

[2] Cross the bridge and follow the track uphill. Just after the bend take the path on the left signed with a marker post. This path heads

across the heather to join another track further up. Continue along this track to pass through a gate in the fence line.

③ At this point look down the fence line to your left and you will see a stile; in winter it is possible to cross this stile and follow the path to a second stile, but in summer the path disappears among high bracken. However, if you continue on the main path you will see the second stile below on your left. You need to cross the second stile and follow an indistinct path high above the Carey Burn valley.

④ Continue on this path and it will begin to follow the fence line of a new wood. When you come to a stile leading into the wood, go over the stile and turn left

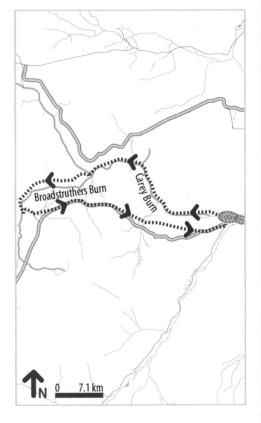

to emerge onto the main track. Follow this track downhill and through a metal gate onto the road. Turn left and walk over the bridge to the parking area.

Points of interest

Up until the end of 2007 it was impossible to walk down the length of the Carey Burn as there was no public right of way. However, on 14 January 2008 a Public Rights of Way Modification Order was granted by Northumberland Council and from this date it has been possible to walk along one of the nicest valleys in the Cheviots.

Happy Valley & North Middleton

START Car parking area north of the Carey Burn Bridge, GR NT975249

NEAREST POSTCODE NE71 6RE

DISTANCE 4½ miles (7.2km)

SUMMARY Easy

MAP OS Explorer OL16 The Cheviot Hills

WHERE TO EAT AND DRINK There are various cafés and pubs in Wooler

A short climb above Happy Valley, with a nice easy descent to North Middleton and a return through Happy Valley. This walk can be combined with the Carey Burn and Broadstruther walk (see above) to create a 9-mile loop.

START Turn right from the parking area, go across the Carey Burn Bridge and turn left at the public footpath sign for Middleton Old Town (1½ miles), North and South Middleton (2 miles). Go through the gate and over the footbridge and follow the path as it begins to climb above Coldgate Water.

1   You will come to a marker post indicating a path leading up the hill and one carrying straight on. Go straight on and the path moves away from the valley onto higher ground. The path then drops into a small valley and picks up a track leading past a large pond with some old bird hides on the opposite side. Follow the track round to the right as it climbs up, with a wood line to your left. The track turns into a path and opens out with the valley below and to your left.

2   Keep straight on with the valley to your left, ignoring any paths leading off left or right. As the path moves away from the valley once more and as you go through a gate and across a stile, you will see the walls of Middleton Old Town in front of you. Look diagonally left down the slope and you will see a stile. Go over it, cross a footbridge and go up and over a second stile. You are now on a well-defined track that leads left downhill towards North Middleton. Go down to the minor road, turn left past North Middleton and continue on the road until just before the ford, where you turn left over the footbridge.

3. Once over the footbridge turn left and continue on the path as it leads through the wood. You are now walking through Happy Valley, which was a popular place for visitors in the early years of the twentieth century. The path comes out into the open and you continue straight ahead, with Coldgate Water on your left-hand side. There is one patch of overgrown gorse to make your way through, but the path continues on until you cross a stile with a public footpath sign pointing back to Colgate Mill (1¾ miles). After crossing the stile, turn left on the road and make your way back to the parking area.

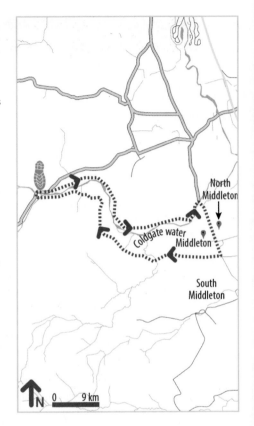

Points of interest

North Middleton: The name 'Middleton' is a very common Old English place name and means 'middle village' or 'middle homestead'. There are many examples of the name in Northumberland.

North Middleton and its neighbour South Middleton are large farms now, but 200 years ago were thriving communities with a population approaching 200 living in over 30 houses. They were mostly employed in sheep farming, but with its decline the residents slowly dispersed.

27 Craster & Dunstanburgh Castle

STARTː Quarry car park, Craster,
GR NU255198

POSTCODE NE66 3TW

DISTANCE 4½ miles (7.2km)

SUMMARY Easy; field tracks and
beach walking

MAP OS Explorer 332 Alnwick &
Amble

WHERE TO EAT AND DRINK The
Jolly Fisherman, Craster, www.
thejollyfishermancraster.co.uk;
Craster Fish Restaurant, Craster,
www.kipper.co.uk/restaurant;
Piper's Pitch, Craster, next to the
Tourist Information Office; Shoreline
Café, Craster

An easy walk from Craster following field tracks and returning along the
beach past Dunstanburgh Castle. This walk can be combined with the
Craster and Howick Hall walk (see below) to create a 9-mile loop.

START Directly across the road from the Quarry car park, take the
track signed for Dunstan Square (1 mile). When you come to a gate
turn left, pass through another gate and head up the hill, keeping
the fence on your left. At Dunstan Square Farm turn right and
follow the concrete farm track, signed Dunstan Steads (1¼ miles).
As you walk along this track look out for the old World War II
pillbox made entirely of sandbags filled with concrete, the sandbags
long since rotted away. These pillboxes are a feature of walks in
Northumberland and were originally put in place against a perceived
threat of invasion from German forces coming across the North Sea
from Norway.

1 At Dunstan Steads head past the cottages and turn right on the
road, heading down towards the coast. When you reach the end of the
road ignore the Coastal Path sign and walk down the track across the
golf course to the beach. If the tide is out, turn right and walk down the
beach; if the tide is in, turn right on the sand dunes above the beach and
follow the track that you will find there. If you follow the beach route, at
some stage the large boulders will defeat your progress and you will find
yourself on the track along the sand dunes.

2 As you approach Dunstanburgh Castle take the track up the side of the embankment to come out facing the main gatehouse. From here back to Craster there is no main path but you really cannot miss the wide expanse of grass leading all the way back to the village. Once in the village, follow the road as it curves to the right and leads you back towards the car park.

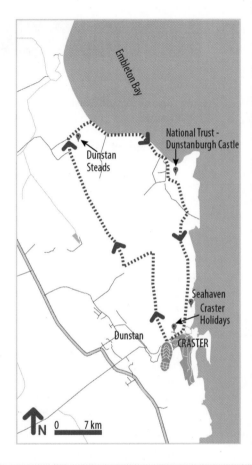

Points of interest

Dunstanburgh Castle: Begun in 1313 by Thomas, second Earl of Lancaster, the Castle was finished or at least operational by 1319. In August 1319 Earl Thomas passed through Dunstanburgh en route to the siege of Berwick – almost certainly the only time that he ever saw his new castle. Never a favourite with the king, Edward II, Thomas was executed in 1322. Now owned by English Heritage, the castle is open at weekends through the winter and daily during the summer months.

Craster & Howick Hall

Start Quarry car park, Craster
GR NU255198

Postcode NE66 3TW

Distance 4½ miles (7.2km)

Summary Easy; field tracks and
beach walking

Map OS Explorer 332 Alnwick &
Amble

Where to eat and drink The
Jolly Fisherman, Craster, www.
thejollyfishermancraster.co.uk;
Craster Fish Restaurant, Craster,
www.kipper.co.uk/restaurant;
Piper's Pitch, Craster, next to the
Tourist Information Office; Shoreline
Café, Craster

An easy walk from Craster following field tracks and returning along the
coastal path. This walk can be combined with the Craster and Dunstanburgh
Castle walk (see above) to create a 9-mile loop.

Start Take the path behind the Tourist Information office. It is signed
Craster South Farm, but the sign may be difficult to see in the summer
due to growing vegetation. Follow this path all the way to the end of
the wooded quarry. Leaving the wooded area behind, head across the
fields until a road reached. Cross the road and follow the minor road
up towards the farm buildings. On the road junction there is a sign for
Howick Hall Gates (1¼ miles). The track leads to the right of the high
ground called Hips Heugh; if you keep to the wall on your right you will
miss the boggy section in the middle of the field.

1 After passing through a gate the track continues over rough ground
and then curves left along a field boundary. The track comes out on the
main track, leading to the car park next to Howick Hall. Continue on
this track to reach the minor road, where you turn left, heading down
towards the coast. Where the road turns sharp left, continue down a
track until you come to the main coastal path and turn left back towards
Craster.

2 Shortly after turning left on the coastal path you will pass a house
perched on the edge of a low cliff. Built in the early nineteenth century

for the second Earl Grey, it was once the bathing house for the family who lived in Howick Hall. As the Earl Grey had 16 children it must have been a popular and noisy place in the summer. The house is now self-catering accommodation.

③ Keep walking along the coastal path until you reach the Jolly Fisherman pub in Craster. Turn left here, cross the road and walk up the minor road called Whin Hill. At the top bear right and then left and follow the track back to the car park.

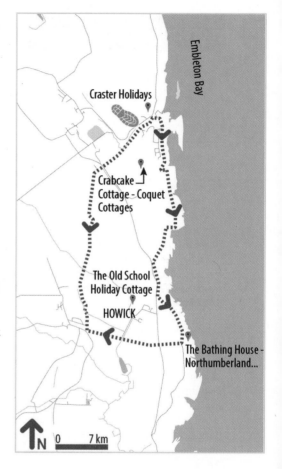

Craster Holidays

Embleton Bay

Crabcake Cottage - Coquet Cottages

The Old School Holiday Cottage

HOWICK

The Bathing House - Northumberland...

N 0   7 km

Points of interest

Howick Hall Gardens: Although the house is not open to the public, the gardens are open nearly all year starting in February with the Snowdrop Festival. There is also the arboretum, all 65 acres of it, holding 11,000 trees and shrubs. Howick Hall Gardens has been rated by BBC Gardeners' World Magazine as one of the top five coastal gardens in the country. Unfortunately it allows assistance dogs only.

29 Ford Village Circular

START Ford village, GR NT947375

NEAREST POSTCODE TD15 2QG

DISTANCE 4½ miles (7.2km)

SUMMARY Easy

MAP OS Explorer 339 Kelso, Coldstream & Lower Tweed Valley

WHERE TO EAT AND DRINK The Restoration Coffee Shop, Ford, T01890-820325 (open Tues–Sun); Heatherslaw Tearoom, T01890-820737, facebook.com/heatherslawtearoom

From Ford village the walk goes to Hay Farm, which is a Heavy Horse Centre (www.hayfarmheavies.co.uk). From the farm the walk goes through farmland and then on a footpath beside the B6354 to Heatherslaw Mill, and returns along the River Till and through the churchyard of St Michael and All Angels back to Ford.

START In Ford village there are some public toilets to the right of the village. At the toilets there is a public footpath sign pointing across the field. Walk across the field to the minor road, turn left and walk to the next marker post that you can see. The marker post is another public footpath sign, indicating a left turn to Hay Farm (½ mile).

1 Go through the gate at the end of the wood and follow the edge of the field to your left. There are quite a few markers on this section of the route, but turn right at the field end and walk towards the farm.

2 Turn left on the farm track past the public footpath sign and into Hay Farm. The farm is home to some heavy horses and you can turn right through the picnic area and continue on a rough grassy path through a gate at the end of the field, across a foot bridge and up the slope on the other side. The original footpath across the field ahead has become difficult to follow, so turn left along the field edge and then right to walk along a strip wood on your left all the way down past the saw mill to exit onto a minor road opposite the Smithy.

3 Turn left down the road to the T-junction, cross the road and

turn left to pick up a public footpath signed to Heatherslaw (½ mile). When you reach Heatherslaw cross the bridge and turn left past the mill buildings. Continue on the road until you reach some cottages on your right-hand side, where you turn left on a public footpath indicating Ford Bridge.

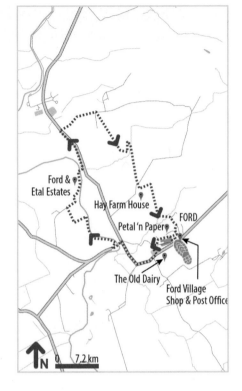

④ The footpath is well marked and follows the River Till on your left-hand side until you reach the B6354, where you turn left to Ford Bridge. Cross the bridge and at the T-junction turn right. There is a footpath on the opposite side of the road that will lead you up the hillside towards Ford village.

⑤ Turn left at the church of St Michael and All Angels and follow the path up to the church. To the left of the church the path continues through a gate with a sign to Ford village. Follow the path as it passes through the grounds of Ford Castle to bring you out into Ford village.

Points of interest

Ford village: Rebuilt after 1859 by Louisa, Marchioness of Waterford, who inherited the estate from her husband. A new school was also built, which is now called Lady Waterford Hall. The building is decorated with wall paintings created by her over a period of 22 years (1860–82). She died in 1891 and is buried in St Michael and All Angels Church.

START Lay-by, north side of Hepple Bridge, GR NT981002

NEAREST POSTCODE NE65 7LL

DISTANCE 4½ miles (7.2km)

SUMMARY Easy; the going is flat except when passing High and Low Farnham

MAP OS Explorer OL16 The Cheviot Hills

WHERE TO EAT AND DRINK The Cross Keys Inn, Thropton, T01669-620362; The Three Wheat Heads Inn, Thropton, www.threewheatheads. co.uk; there are also more pubs and cafés in Rothbury

Good views along Coquetdale on the way out and then views across to the Simonside Hills on the return. The route covers some of the Sandstone Way, which is a recent (2014) 100-mile cycle route from Berwick to Hexham.

START From the start at the lay-by, turn north on the road away from the bridge and a short distance along the road on the left is a public footpath sign indicating West Hepple (¼ mile). Turn left here and walk up the hillside, heading towards the right-hand corner of the group of trees where there is a stile.

① Cross the stile, turn left on the track and follow it into the farmyard at West Hepple. In the top right corner there is a marker on a fence post. Follow the track around to the left behind the barns and just past the last barn turn right along a track that has a marker for the Border Country Ride. Follow the track as it turns left and then right alongside a wood, going steadily downhill.

② As you walk downhill there is a marker post in the centre of a field. The markers have worn away, but turn diagonally left and walk down to the wood line to pass through two gates on the edge of the wood. After the second gate turn left and walk along the edge of the wood until it ends, where you go left through a gate, crossing a bridge over a stream.

③ Turn right and continue on the path with the fence line on your right, ignoring any tracks or stiles on your right, until you come to a wooden gate set at an angle to the fence line. Go through the gate and up the rise to pass through a wood and out onto a minor road, where you turn right.

④ Continue along the road, passing High Farnham and Low Farnham Cottages. As the road turns sharp left at Low Farnham go straight ahead on the track. It has a public footpath sign indicating Caistron (1½ miles). As you approach the buildings at Wreighill, take the right turn on a track that takes you past the barns on your right. At the T-junction turn right and continue on the track until it makes a sharp turn to the right. In front of you is a gate, which you go through, and then continue downhill on the grassy track until it emerges on the road at Hepple. Turn right and continue along the road a short way to arrive back at the lay-by.

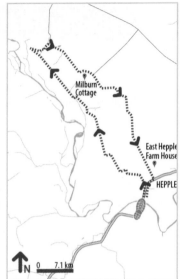

Points of interest

Many of the villages in this part of Northumbria were subject to raids by the Border Reivers, but none more so than the village of Wreighill. On 25 May 1415, in retaliation for continued opposition to previous raids, the village was attacked and burnt, and most of the villagers were killed.

Although the village was rebuilt and once more occupied, it was decimated again in 1665 when the plague came to the village and killed most of the inhabitants. The village never really recovered after that and by the turn of the nineteenth century there were no more than 30 people living there. By 1900 the village had all but disappeared and was replaced by a farm that still bears the original name.

No mention is made on modern Ordnance Survey maps, but if you look at an aerial image the remains of the village can be seen to the north of the farm.

Sinderhope & Low Acton

START High Forest Community Centre, Sinderhope (just off the B6295), GR NY845520

DISTANCE 4½ miles (7.2km)

SUMMARY Moderate. A lovely walk with good views over fields and along quiet roads

MAP OS Explorer OL43 Hadrian's Wall

WHERE TO EAT AND DRINK There are various pubs and cafés in Allendale Town, including small speciality shops

START From the Community Centre entrance cross the B6295 and go over the stile. Walk up the field, going diagonally right, and at the top of the rise you will see an old ruin. Walk past the ruin and turn right along the wall line. Walk in front of the building at High Sinderhope and go over the ladder stile, cross the track and follow the track that leads past the barn on your right. Go over another wall stile and across the field to exit through a gate in the right-hand corner of the field.

1   Turn left on the road and continue along it until you turn right on the minor road that zigzags down the hill to cross a footbridge over the river. Continue along this road until you turn right at the next minor road. As this road bends to the right, after the bridge over a stream look for a footpath sign on your right. The sign indicates Pry Hill; go through the gate and continue on the path above the stream. Cross the stile on the left before Knockburn Farm and head right through a gap in the wall and down to a gate in the fence line in front of you. Turn left after the gate and follow the path beside the fence to go over a bridge across a stream and then over a ladder stile beside a large tree.

2   The path leads down and past the bastle of Rowantree Stob. Cross the footbridge and head left down towards the main bridge over the river. Do not cross it but take the small footbridge to the left. Follow the footpath and cross several wall stiles and gates to pass between the farm buildings at Pry Hill. Turn right on the minor road and then almost immediately turn left at a public footpath sign that indicates Peckriding (2 miles).

③ Walk across the field with the fence line to your right, cross a stile and head diagonally left towards the trees. There is a marker post just before the tree line and then steps that take you down into the valley. Walk across the boards and over the bridge, then climb the slope on the other side but turn left as you climb.

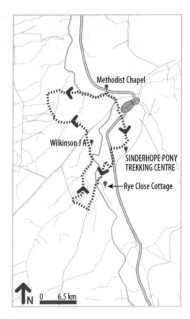

④ There is no obvious path here, but climb up towards the farm of Low Acton, and as you approach the rear of the barns there is a concrete walkway that leads out into the farmyard. Turn half-right and go through the gate that leads out of the farm; there is a stile on the right through another gate but it is easy to miss. Once out of the farm head across the field, keeping the next set of farm building to your left.

⑤ Cross two farm ditches, one with a footbridge, and keep going across the fields until you come to a main farm track, where you turn right and pass between the buildings of Crowberry Hall. Follow the path with the stream and fence line to your left, go through a gate and across the bridge, and continue across the field towards a finger-post that you can see in front of you. The finger-post indicates Parks to your left, Pry Hill to the right, and to your rear is Crowberry. Take the indicator straight ahead to Holms Linn, going downhill and towards the river. Be aware that most of the walk boards are broken and dangerous and, depending on the time of year, the whole area is muddy underfoot.

⑥ Walk past the mine workings of Holms Linn and cross the footbridge over the river close to a fine waterfall. Turn right and follow the path as it climbs up to the stile at the minor road. Cross the road and over another stile that is signed to the Community Centre.

⑦ Walk up the slope, keeping close to the stream running downhill, and look for a stile on the right that is in the bend of the fence line on the far side of the stream. Cross the stile, turn left over another stile and walk up the field to enter the rear yard of the Community Centre.

Spartylea & High Knock Shield

START Spartylea, GR NY850489
POSTCODE: NE47 9UA

DISTANCE 4½ miles (7.2km)

SUMMARY Moderate

MAPS OS Explorer OL31 North
Pennines and OS Explorer OL43
Hadrian's Wall

WHERE TO EAT AND DRINK There are
various pubs and cafés in Allendale
Town, including small speciality
shops

PARKING Just of the B6295 in the
parking area by the old Post Office

Leaving Spartylea alongside the River East Allen, the route heads upstream
past the remains of old mine workings to return via the old miners' road
called the Black Way, which now forms part of Isaac's Tea Trail.

START From the parking area walk downhill on the minor road and turn
right after crossing the bridge over the River East Allen. Follow the track
until it bears left and then continue on the path beside the river. Walk
alongside the river until you cross a footbridge, where you turn left, and
continue with the river now on your left.

1 The path turns into a minor road at the buildings of Tedham Green
and starts to bear away from the river and climb slowly uphill, passing
some old mine workings and cottages on your left-hand side. Just
past the cottages take the left turn on a track to head down to a small
footbridge. After the bridge cross a track to continue on a footpath,
taking the left-hand fork of the Y-junction. Just after the Y-junction
there is a small sign on the right that indicates an alternative path, which
bypasses the house below.

2 Continue on the alternative path with trees on your right until you
come to a wall directly ahead of you. Turn left here and head downhill to
pick up the original path, where you turn right to head through the trees
to pick up the river again on your left-hand side. Continue alongside the
river, crossing several stiles, until you reach the end of the wood, where
you turn left to cross a footbridge over the river

3 After crossing the footbridge, continue on the minor road called Black Way, which also forms part of Isaac's Tea Trail. Follow this road, ignoring the public footpath sign on your left that indicates Spartylea (1¼ miles). At High Knock Shield the road turns into a track as you go through a gate. Continue straight on past the T-junction, where there are marker posts indicating the way. Just past the T-junction Isaac's Tea Trail bears off to your right, but continue on the main track. As you approach the wall that is coming downhill on your right, turn left on the path that is heading towards the gate to the right of the house. Go through the gate and continue across the field, with the fence line to your right.

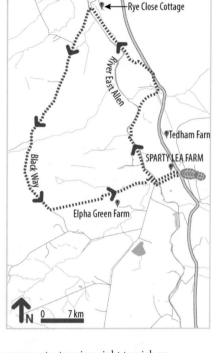

4 Pass through several gates to come out on the track by the house at Elpha Green. Continue on the track until you go through one more gate, turning right to pick up the original route that will lead back to the parking area.

Points of interest

On the return journey along the Black Way the route goes past the farm at High Knock Shield. The meadow at grid reference 838502 has been designated a Site of Special Scientific Interest. As a traditionally managed upland hay meadow, this field is a remnant of a habitat that was once widespread in northern England, but is now scarce due to modern intensive agricultural methods. The field is notable for having more than 20 varieties of flowers and grasses.

33 Walltown & the Vallum

START Small parking area alongside the road, GR NY674661

MAP OS Explorer OL43 Hadrian's Wall

NEAREST POSTCODE CA8 7HF

DISTANCE 4½ miles (7.2km)

SUMMARY Hard. This walk can be extended using the Walltown and Thirlwall Castle walk (Walk 24) to create a loop of 8½ miles

WHERE TO EAT AND DRINK There is a shop at Walltown Quarry Visitor Centre and a café at the Roman Army Museum

Starting from the parking area close to Walltown Quarry Visitor Centre, the walk heads eastwards over Walltown Crags to follow the Roman Wall as far as Aesica Roman Fort, before returning along the course of the Vallum.

START From the car park walk diagonally uphill to the right to reach Walltown Crags. Turn right and follow the path as it descends to cross a stile and climbs the steps to regain the height on the other side of the pass. The path continues along the top, rising and falling as it follows the contours of the ridge line. After passing through a wood, you will pass the farm at Cockmount Hill and beyond you will see the outline of Aesica Roman Fort, whose modern name is Great Chesters.

1 Turn right on the path leading down from the farm and pass an altar stone, before going through the farm gate and turning right. The altar stone nearly always has a pile of coins on top of it. Continue down the clear track that follows the course of the Vallum, which was a defensive ditch – this part now hidden under the track. Continue along the track as it curves right and passes a rather large lime kiln on the right-hand side. The path continues on and passes Walltown Farm and shortly after will bring you back to the parking area.

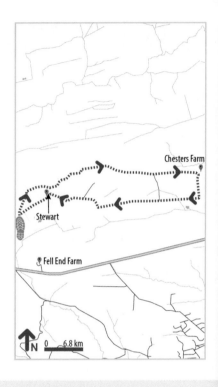

Points of interest

Walltown Visitor Centre is open Apr–end Oct and has a small shop. The toilets are open all year round. Walks led by a National Park Ranger are held here over the summer. The car park has parking charges. Close by and only a short walk away is the Carvoran Roman Army Museum, based on the site of Magnis Roman Fort. There is a car park at the museum, which has an entrance fee but is well worth visiting. The museum is open all year except for the months of Dec and Jan.

Aesica Roman Fort was built to guard Caw Gap just over a mile away to the east. In its lifetime the fort was guarded by auxiliary soldiers from modern-day Belgium and Switzerland. The fort was excavated in 1897 and one noticeable feature was the construction of bathhouses fed by aqueducts running for six miles to the north of the wall.

Wooler & Weetwood Moor

Start Car park near Glendale Tea Room and Garden Centre, Wooler, GR NT994279

Nearest postcode NE71 6QD

Distance 4½ miles (7.2km)

Summary Moderate

Map OS Explorer 340 Holy Island & Bamburgh

Where to eat and drink There are various cafés and pubs in Wooler

A nice, easy climb to the top of Weetwood Moor with some great views of the surrounding countryside, including the Cheviot Hills.

Start From the parking area walk back to the minor road and turn left. You are on part of St Cuthbert's Way as it heads north-east on the last 18 miles (29km) to Holy Island. Continue along the road, going uphill, and as the road swings right take the waymarked track with the St Cuthbert's Way sign on your left.

[1] When you reach the top of the hill there is a Y-junction. The left-hand path is a continuation of St Cuthbert's Way; ignore this and take the right-hand path. As you clear the brow of the hill and look ahead, the perspective and distance make it look as if there are three woods ahead of you. Stay on the path that is leading towards the right-hand corner of the middle wood. There are other paths crossing the moor but continue on the sometimes indistinct path, passing an old marker sign along the way.

[2] As you approach the wood you will come to a small ditch. At this point if you look to your right you will see a stile crossing the fence line. You need to make your way to the stile, cross it and continue on the path going diagonally left. The path leads to a gate, which you go through, and then follow the path with the white marker posts down to the minor road. Here, there is a public footpath sign pointing back to Weetwood Moor (½ mile) and Wooler (2¼ miles).

[3] Turn right on the minor road and continue along it, ignoring the left turn in the wood. The road will become a track, and as the track bears left at a small wood there is a gate on the right-hand side. Go

through the gate and walk down the hill past a wood on your right, with a quick view of one of the Coldmartin Loughs, to exit through a gate onto a well-defined track, where you turn right.

④ The track becomes a tarmac road just before the entrance to the Radio Station, which is on the right. On the left-hand side there is a public footpath sign indicating Coldmartin (¼ mile); turn left here. Walk past the Scout Camp and go through a gate in the wall on the left.

⑤ Continue down the hill and go through a second gate and then diagonally left across the field. Before the next gate bear right downhill. As the telegraph poles angle away to the right, continue down the hillside to cross a ladder stile over the wall among the gorse bushes. Once over the ladder stile continue downhill, going through a gate in the middle of the fence line.

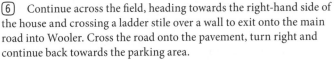

⑥ Continue across the field, heading towards the right-hand side of the house and crossing a ladder stile over a wall to exit onto the main road into Wooler. Cross the road onto the pavement, turn right and continue back towards the parking area.

Points of interest

Weetwood Moor may look a little lonely as you cross it, with the odd person or group heading along St Cuthbert's Way or the occasional person walking on one of the paths that cross the moor. But for some 500 years until the nineteenth century, a market was held on the moor every Whit weekend, where cattle, sheep and horses were for sale and servants could be hired. The Ordnance Survey map still lists the hill as Whitsunbank Hill.

35 Humbleton Hill & Wooler Common

START Car Park at Humbleton Burn, GR NT976272

NEAREST POSTCODE NE71 6PB

DISTANCE 4¾ miles (7.6km)

SUMMARY Moderate; bridleways and footpaths on the edge of the Cheviots

MAP OS Explorer OL16 The Cheviot Hills

WHERE TO EAT AND DRINK There are various cafés and pubs in Wooler

A moderate walk around the lower slopes of Humbleton Hill on the edge of the Cheviot Hills, with wide-ranging views. There is an optional diversion that climbs to the top of Humbleton Hill.

START From the car park walk behind the information board on an asphalt track, go past the dog loop sign and turn left through the wood, where a sign for St Cuthbert's Way indicates the direction uphill. At the top of the hill go through a gate and continue straight on. Go through a gate at the end of the track and turn right. Go through a second gate and follow a stony track downhill until you reach a gate on the left with a public bridleway sign indicating Gleadscleugh (1½ miles); turn left here.

1 Cross a stile and continue on the bridleway, ignoring a right-branching track, until you come to a waymarker with a public footpath and Hill Fort Trail pointing straight ahead. Continue on the public footpath until you reach another gate and stile, which you go through and over, and turn left to follow a narrow footpath as it climbs through a valley between Harehope Hill and Humbleton Hill. Ignore the left fork that will lead you up Humbleton Hill (but see the diversion note below – final paragraph).

2 Continue along this footpath until a T-junction and waymarker are reached. Turn left here and as the footpath descends down the hillside it swings left to join another T-junction with a gate to the left. Do not go through the gate, but instead turn right.

3 Go through the gate at the end of the footpath and descend

diagonally right to approach a minor road. A gate leads you onto the road where you turn left, following the road until you reach a marker post on the right indicating Broadstruther (2½ miles); turn right onto the grassy track and over a footbridge.

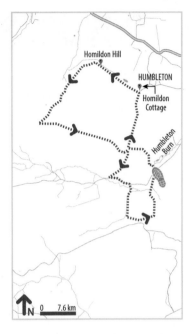

④   After the footbridge go through a gate, cross a small stream and turn right on the grassy track. The track appears to come to an end in the corner of a field, but turn left up a small incline and the track opens up again as it comes close to the rear of the farm at Wooler Common. Continue past the farm and as you approach a wall turn left; a short way along this track is a waymarker with a sign for St Cuthbert's Way and a public bridleway sign pointing diagonally left. Take the public bridleway as it leads over rough pasture down to a gate that leads along the edge of a wood, then out onto a minor road, where you can see the car park ahead of you.

⑤   An interesting diversion on this walk is to climb Humbleton Hill from the valley between Humbleton and Harehope Hills. As you walk up the narrow valley there is a left fork in the track and a stile to climb over before getting on the permissive path that leads upwards, with a ravine on your right-hand side. Although the path is steep, the views from the top are spectacular. A well-marked track leads down from the top to a gate where you turn right, picking up the original route after passing through two more gates.

Points of interest

Humbleton Hill: The top of the hill contains the impressive remains of an Iron Age fort, which would have been protected with a high rampart wall that now lies in ruins at the top of the hill.

Holy Island Circular

START Holy Island car park,
GR NU126424

POSTCODE TD15 2SE

DISTANCE 5 miles (8km)

SUMMARY Easy

MAP OS Explorer 340 Holy Island &
Bamburgh

WHERE TO EAT AND DRINK There are
various pubs and cafés on Holy
Island

This route does an easy loop around Holy Island on well-defined tracks and
footpaths. It can easily be extended or shortened as required. It could take a
full day to complete if visits were made to the Priory and the Castle en route
and an exploration of the village on the return.

START From the car park turn left on the road and walk into the village.
Follow the road to the right and then left as it leads down to Lindisfarne
Priory. After visiting the Priory retrace your steps and turn right after
the Visitor Centre. Walk down to the gap between the house and the
wall, pass through an old turnstile and follow the path to the south side
of the island.

1 Follow the path down to the bay and walk between the upturned
boats to leave the bay on a tarmac track. Follow the track past
Lindisfarne Castle, which you can visit, and continue on the path closest
to the sea past the lime kilns to the farthest southern tip of the island.
Turn north and follow the path past all the rock art and head towards
the white pyramid on Emmanuel Head.

2 Continue on the path past the pyramid and head towards Sandham
Bay. Walk across the bay to exit on the far side. When you reach what
looks like a gully but is in fact a shelf of land that has been exposed to
the sea, turn left and follow it inland. When you can see the painted
marker posts, follow them through the dunes and they will lead to a gate
on the edge of the nature reserve.

3 Go through the gate and continue on the path as it heads back

towards the village. Turn right past the coach and disabled parking area and turn right at the T-junction to walk back to the car park. Alternatively turn left at the T-junction to further explore the village.

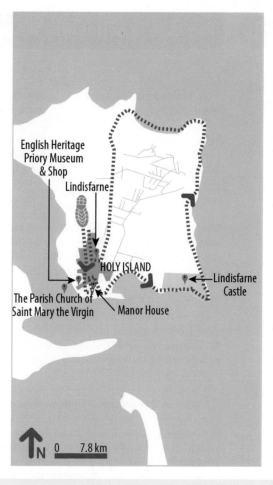

English Heritage Priory Museum & Shop

Lindisfarne

HOLY ISLAND

The Parish Church of Saint Mary the Virgin

Manor House

Lindisfarne Castle

N   0   7.8 km

Points of interest

Emmanuel Head: The white brick pyramid called a navigation daymark was built sometime between 1801 and 1810. It is 35ft high and is positioned on a small cliff some 10ft high. Its purpose is to provide a daylight navigational aid for seamen on the approach to Holy Island.

Ros Castle & Ros Hill Wood

Start Hepburn Woods car park, GR NU071247

Nearest postcode NE66 4EG

Distance 5 miles (8km)

Summary Moderate

Map OS Explorer 332 Alnwick & Amble

Where to eat and drink The Tankerville Arms, Eglingham, www.tankervillearms.com

First, there is a short climb out of Hepburn Woods through some crags to an obvious hill fort. Then the route continues across the heather to another climb to the top of Ros Castle; the hill fort here is not so obvious. The return is via heather moor and woodland and along a short stretch of minor road.

Start From the car park take the track into the wood, but after the metal barrier look for a path on the left heading up through the trees. The path leads to a ladder stile and then up through large boulders and into the remains of a hill fort. Follow the path through the hill fort and across the heather as it leads you to the minor road.

1⃝   On the opposite side of the road is the path that leads uphill to the trig point on Ros Castle. After taking in the viewpoint, follow the path to the right, which is close to the wall and heads down to the wood. Continue on the path between the wall and the wood and you will come to a boundary stone marked with the date 1859. The wall turns to the left here, but continue on the path between the fences. The wood to your left has been felled so there are good views across the country to the coast.

2⃝   Continue on the path until you reach a broken gate on your right with a Forestry Commission marker indicating a right turn. Turn right and follow a broad path through the trees until you come to a clearing; cross the clearing and go left to pick up the path after crossing a small stream. The path comes out at a fence line on the far side of the woods, where you turn right, passing another boundary

stone and heading slowly
uphill.

③ The path curves right,
following the side of the wood,
and as you come opposite
the large aerial mast on your
left there is a clearing on
your right. Turn right here
and follow the path as it goes
through the clearing. When
you come to the T-junction
turn left; later the path goes
through another clearing and
then back into the wood for a
short distance before exiting
the woods over a stile.

④ Continue straight ahead
past a small wood on your left
to reach the minor road that
you crossed earlier. Turn right
and walk down the road back
to Hepburn Woods car park.

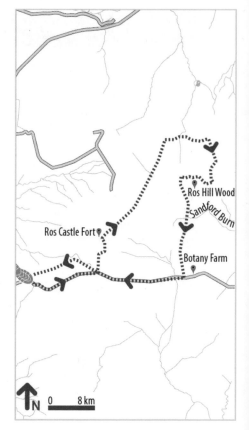

Points of interest

Ros Castle: On the summit of Ros Castle is an Iron Age hill fort,
and it is the highest point of a low range of hills stretching from
Alnwick to Berwick-upon-Tweed. The summit is marked by a trig
point and nearby there is a rather unusual walk-in toposcope built into the
wall with four separate plaques. The view is panoramic and very extensive,
and on a clear day a total of seven castles can be seen from the summit,
including the one on Holy Island.

START Simonside car park,
GR NZ036996

NEAREST POSTCODE NE65 7NW

DISTANCE 5 miles (8km)

SUMMARY Strenuous; through
woodland and then a climb onto
the Simonside Hills, a great ridge
walk and then a gentle descent back
down to the car park

MAP OS Explorer OL42 Kielder
Water & Forest

WHERE TO EAT AND DRINK The closest
town for refreshments is Rothbury

Starting from the woodland car park at Simonside, the route makes its way
through woodland and then up and along the ridge of the Simonside Hills,
with panoramic views of Coquetdale and the Cheviot Hills.

START From the car park walk back to the main information board
and take the right-hand track, following the red waymarkers. The
track makes its way through the wood, going steadily uphill. At the
T-junction take the right-hand track and at the Y-junction take the
left-hand track; the red waymarkers are still in place. On this section
of track look out for two rocks on the left just before a cleared area of
woodland; there is a path on the left that will lead you to Little Church
Rock, where it is believed that in medieval times church preachings
were held.

1   Once you have visited Little Church Rock, return to the main
track and continue until you come to a Y-junction, where you take the
left-hand track. This track used to be much wider than it is now and you
may notice the man-made markings on a large rock as you walk over it.
Continue on this track, keeping left at the next red waymarker. The track
leaves the wood and crosses over heather and bracken to come out on a
main track, where you turn right.

2   At the T-junction turn left and left again to the information board,

before climbing the short but steep section up onto Simonside. When you reach the top there is a footpath that you follow that runs all along the top of this short range of hills. There are occasional red marker posts indicating the way.

(3) As you drop down a set of stone flagged steps you will see the red marker posts indicating a route down on the left-hand side. Ignore the route and continue down the steps and you will see a fence line with a gate. Beyond the gate on the left-hand side you will see a path going through the heather; this is the path where you leave the hillside.

(4) The path is rough at first but it does turn into a paved path a little lower down. The paved section turns into a section of steps; where these steps end turn and look back and you will see that you have just made your way through a break in a wall. This was once part of the thirteenth-century Deer Park Wall; in the year 1310 it was described as having a perimeter of a 'league' (approximately 3 miles) in length.

(5) In winter, if you keep the fence line on your left close by, you can descend on a path that leads down to the road below; however, in summer this path is overgrown and difficult to see, so keep on the main path and descend to the minor road, where you turn left and walk back to the car park.

Points of interest

Little Church Rock is believed to have been used for church meetings in medieval times.

The ridge of Simonside Hills offers great views and ancient burial cairns.

39 Spartylea & Swinhope

START Spartylea, GR NY850489

POSTCODE NE47 9UA

DISTANCE 5 miles (8km)

SUMMARY Moderate. A pleasant walk by the riverside, along quiet roads and over fields, through a former lead mining area

MAP OS Explorer OL31 North Pennines

WHERE TO EAT AND DRINK There are various pubs and cafés in Allendale Town, including small speciality shops

Parking Just off the B6295 in the parking area by the old Post Office

The walk heads out of Spartylea to follow the River East Allen upstream, before climbing away from the river close to the village of Dirt Pot and returning through the pleasant side valley of Swinhope.

START From the parking area walk back uphill to the junction with the B6295 and in the right-hand corner of the junction there is a public footpath sign that will lead you over a ladder stile and across a field. Keep to the high ground until you reach the next stile, as the lower ground is boggy. After crossing the stile continue on past a ruined building and over a footbridge. Keep to the right and follow the path up to a gate leading out onto a minor road, where you turn right over a bridge. Just before the Chapel turn left at the public footpath sign that indicates Peasmeadows (1 mile) and Dirt Pot (1¾ miles).

① Continue along the riverside path, ignoring the footbridges over the river. Cross a footbridge over a stream and continue on with the path beginning to move away from the river to the right. As a gate comes into view that leads onto a minor road, turn sharply right on a track leading almost back the way you have come.

② Cross a bridge and just before the cottage cross a wall stile, and walk over a field to cross another wall stile. Climb the rise before the farm at Hammershield, crossing the farm road over two wall stiles with a public footpath sign indicating Swinhope (¾ mile). Keep going diagonally left across the fields, crossing a number of stiles, until you come to a gate with a visible marker post that leads out onto a minor road.

3 Directly opposite there is a track with two public footpath signs, the one on the left indicates High Hope (1 mile) and the one on the right indicates Swinhope Shield (½ mile) and High Moss House (½ mile). Regardless of the indicators, take the left-hand track and stay close to the wall line on your right until you come to a ladder stile, which you go over. Head across the field and through a gate, and just past the telegraph pole with the marker turn right to cross two ladder stiles, turning left to cross a stile at the bottom of the field.

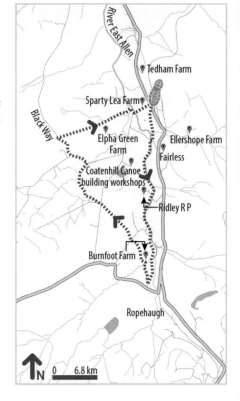

4 Once over the stile head diagonally right across the field to a marker sign on the bridge over the stream at Swinhope Mill. Cross the footbridge and turn sharp right to pass in front of the mill and continue ahead to a Y-junction, taking the left-hand fork which leads left onto a minor road. The road curves left past an old quarry and continues past two cottages on the right. Just after the second cottage turn right on the track that has a sign for Lot Head. At the Y-junction turn left and, where the wall on your left turns sharply left, turn right on the path that leads over grass and is heading towards the gate to the right of the house. Go through the gate and continue across the field with the fence line to your right.

5 Pass through several gates to come out on the track by the house at Elpha Green. Continue on the track until you go through one more gate, turning right over a bridge to meet a minor road. Turn left on the road and walk up the hill to the parking area.

START Bulbys Wood car park,
GR NU008163

NEAREST POSTCODE NE66 4LT

DISTANCE 5 miles (8km)

SUMMARY Moderate. A climb to the
first hillfort and then a fairly easy
gradient to the highest one on
Cochrane Pike. The uphill sections
are worth it for the views and the
experience of walking among the
hill forts

MAP OS Explorer OL16 The Cheviot
Hills

WHERE TO EAT AND DRINK Plough Inn,
Powburn, To1665-578769; Queens
Head, Glanton, To1665-578324;
Poachers Rest, Hedgeley Services,
To1665-578664

A steady uphill walk to the first hill fort on Brough Law. There is a shortcut on
the way to the next hill fort, but to get the best from this walk it is far better
to continue and visit all four of the other hill forts, which are each in their
own unique location.

START From the car park walk across the road to pick up a path next to
the finger-post that indicates the start of the Hillfort Trail and Brough
Law (¾ mile). The path heads uphill past the wood, right to the top of the
hill to the first hill fort called Brough Law. On the left-hand side of the
hill fort you will see a marker post indicating the path that leads away
from the hill fort.

1 On this part of the route you will come to a marker post indicating
a short cut to your left; ignore it and continue on the main path. The
path meets a fence line on your left and as you carry on down the hillside
you reach a stile on your left, where you cross the fence line. You are now
at the second hill fort, Middle Dean. On the right-hand side of this hill
fort there is a finger-post pointing the way down into the valley and then
up the path on the other side.

2 When you reach the broad grassy path the route bears right and,

with marker posts showing the way, you climb steadily to the top of Cochrane Pike. There is a marker post indicating a left turn near the top of the hill, but continue forward some 200yds to reach the hill fort, where you can make out the raised ramparts of the third hill fort. This is also a good position to see down and across the valley where other hill forts are hidden behind the bulk of Old Fawdon Hill.

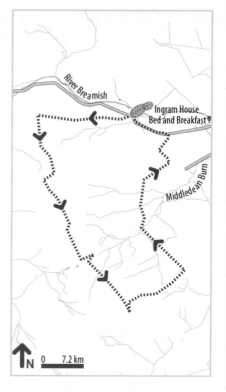

3 Return to the last marker post and take the direction indicated to the fourth hill fort of Wether Hill. From this hill fort head down into the valley with the narrow gully to your left-hand side. At the bottom of the valley go through the gate and head uphill to your right, where you will come to a marker post that indicates the other end of the short cut that you passed earlier. The other direction on the marker post leads off right on a wide path that takes you to the fifth hill fort on Ingram Hill. Walk round the ramparts of this hill fort and then join the track that leads away left down to the road. Turn left on the road and walk back to the car park.

Points of interest

Hill forts are a feature of the Cheviots; wherever you walk there seems to be one not far away. On this relatively short walk there is the opportunity to visit five individual hill forts, each one offering some great views and each one giving a different perspective of the Breamish Valley.

Thrunton Woods & Castle Hill

Start Thrunton Woods Forest car park, GR NU085097

Nearest postcode NE66 4RZ

Distance 5 miles (8km)

Summary Moderate

Map OS Explorer 332 Alnwick & Amble

Where to eat and drink Thrunton Woods is off the main A697 road, to the north is Powburn (the Plough Inn) and south is Longframlington (The Granby Inn)

The route heads out across farmland but soon returns to the woods, with a pleasant walk through the trees climbing up to Castle Hill. The top of the hill is covered in ancient beech trees and is a place worth spending some time looking around. The return involves a very steep climb up through trees and rocks to the top of Callaly Crag, but it must be one of the nicest climbs in Northumberland.

Start Turn left onto the minor road as you leave the car park and continue past the T-junction as the road turns into a stony track. At the Y-junction take the right-hand fork through a gate; initially the track follows the tree line on your left but gradually moves away from it. Go across the fields through gates and the track becomes grass as it start to climb the slope.

① As you reach a gate on your right there is a raised track in front of you; walk up onto it and turn left to follow it to the wood line, where you go over a stile. After crossing the stile, turn left on the track to your front and follow it as it makes a bend through the wood. As the track straightens look out for a grass cross track, where you turn right. This is now a long, straight track going slowly uphill. At its end you reach a T-junction with a main track and almost opposite is a gate set in a wall, which you go through.

② Follow the path to the left past some rhododendron bushes and just past the bushes take the left fork at the Y-junction and follow the path uphill to the top of Castle Hill, where there is a grove of beech trees. After exploring Castle Hill head through the rocky gully on the rear side of the hill to reach a path, where you turn left.

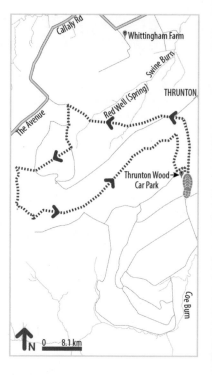

③ This path will drop fairly steeply downhill and then begin to level out, although it is still going downhill, until you reach a line of fence posts where it leads through the trees to a stile. Go over the stile and start the very steep climb to the top of the hill. The path leads through heather and grass and up past large rocks. See if you can spot Macartney's Cave on the way up, although it is easy to miss it if you are concentrating on the climb.

④ When you reach the top, walk out towards the clearing where there is a pond to your right. The path leads away to your left and can sometimes be a bit boggy. The path continues through a gate in a wall, where you turn right. At the T-junction turn left; the path widens out into a track with Thrunton Crags on your left. Ignore the branch tracks to your right as you walk along, until the way ahead becomes narrower. Swing right on the track as it goes over the brow of the hill and then down to meet a main track. Turn left and walk into the car park.

Points of interest

Castle Hill: This is the site of an Iron Age hill fort but whatever remains has quietly disappeared among the surrounding woodland. However, the top of the hill, with the twisted roots and trunks of large beech trees, is a great place to explore.

Macartney's Cave: A hand-made cave created by a chaplain of Callally Castle as a retreat in the nineteenth century.

Morpeth & Bothal

START Whorral Bank lay-by parking area on the A197, GR NZ203864

POSTCODE NNE61 3AA

DISTANCE 5½ miles (9km)

SUMMARY Moderate. A riverside path to Bothal that meanders through a wood, returning mostly over fields

MAP OS Explorer 325 Morpeth & Blyth

WHERE TO EAT AND DRINK There are various pubs and cafés in Morpeth

A walk along a nice easy stretch of the River Wansbeck east of Morpeth, although there are two short uphill sections. If the stepping stones are a problem, the route can be shortened by going across Bothal Bridge.

START Turn left and cross the road after leaving the lay-by parking area. Walk uphill past the right turn over a bridge, which is the way back, and turn right at the public footpath sign that indicates Bothal (2½ miles); there is also an information board at this point.

[1] Continue along the path under the railway viaduct and you will come to some picnic benches and another information board. A short way beyond the benches is the Jubilee Well and the remains of the Lady's Chapel. Continue on past the remains of a mill and parking area and turn left on the road; to the right is Bothal Bridge. At the T-junction continue straight on towards Bothal Castle, which you can see over the hedge.

[2] At the War Memorial turn right past the church and take the public footpath leading down to the River Wansbeck. To cross the river there is a set of wide concrete stepping stones; once across, go up the bank and turn right on a minor road, going uphill. At the T-junction turn right on the minor road. As the road bends to the left there is an unmarked path leading off to the right through the woods. Turn right and follow the path, which will bring you out at Bothal Bridge. You might notice here the rather odd World War II gun

emplacement on this side of the bridge.

③ Turn left and follow the road uphill away from the bridge. As the road bends left go over the stile on the right, with the public footpath indicating Park House (1¼ miles). Continue on the path as it skirts several fields and then re-enters the wood, heading down to and across a bridge over a stream, before bearing right and coming out into open fields on the approach to Park House.

④ Continue past Park House on the minor road and turn right at the public footpath sign that indicates Whorral Bank (¾ mile). The path goes over the railway line and heads down a bankside to a wide bridge that you cross to emerge on the A197, where you turn left and walk back to the lay-by parking area.

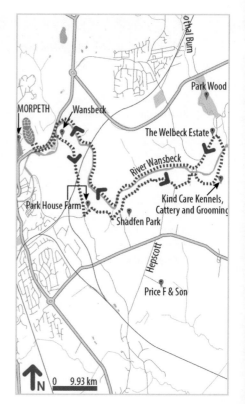

Points of interest

Lady's Chapel: This now ruined chapel lies between the start of the route and Bothal. Not much remains except moss-covered stones and one or two stone courses of the original building. The chapel was in existence on a map of 1610 and there is evidence to suggest it was there in the 1500s and probably used as a chantry. Close by the chapel is the 1887 Jubilee Well, which was constructed for the 60th anniversary of Queen Victoria's accession to the throne, although this also lies as a ruin.

Newbiggin, the Wansbeck & the Art Trail

START Church Point car park, Newbiggin, GR NZ317880

DISTANCE 5½ miles (9km)

SUMMARY Easy

MAP OS Explorer 325 Morpeth & Blyth

WHERE TO EAT AND DRINK There are various pubs and cafés in Newbiggin

Starting from the Maritime Centre, the route heads out of Newbiggin along the curve of the bay. It then continues along a clifftop path, passes through Sandy Bay Caravan Park and out along the beach to where the River Wansbeck joins the sea. The return is similar, but the route goes through the main part of Newbiggin past many exhibits on the Art Trail.

START From the car park head towards St Bartholomew's Church and then turn right onto the promenade next to the Maritime Centre. You can pick up a leaflet for the Art Trail at the Maritime Centre, as many of the pieces of art can be seen on your way round Newbiggin.

① From the Maritime Centre follow the lower promenade all the way round the bay until it drops down into Spital Burn, with Spital Point to your left.

② The path continues behind an old chain-link fence across the other side of Spital Burn and goes up onto the clifftop path. The original public footpath has fallen into the sea along with much of the clifftop, but there is a path that is set back from the cliffs that works its way alongside a field. As you come to the caravan park, go over the stile to your right and make your way between the caravans until you come to the access road leading down to the beach.

③ Turn right and walk along the beach until you reach the very wide river outlet for the River Wansbeck. If the tide is out it is possible to walk down to the river itself across the sand, but this is as far as you can go unless you walk inland, following the course of the river upstream.

④ From this point return through the caravan park and back along

the clifftop path until you reach
Spital Burn. Continue straight over
onto the tarmac path and carry
on walking until you reach the
bowling green. Turn right behind
the bowling green clubhouse and
follow the road round to the left
and then right to come out on
Gibson St, which curves round
the town, changing its name to
Front St and then High St before it
arrives back at the car park.

⑤   As you walk along this one
curving street, there are many
opportunities to turn off through
the side streets to follow the Art
Trail.

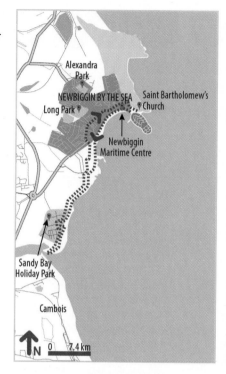

Points of interest

Newbiggin-by-the-Sea: Once important as a port for the shipping
of grain and later as a coal-mining area, Newbiggin was an affluent
town right into the middle of the mid-twentieth century. It was an
attractive place to visit from the industrial areas surrounding Newcastle-
upon-Tyne, and its architecture – particularly along the promenade – shows
that wealthy people made it their home or summer residence.

Newbiggin Art Trail: Started in 2007, this is a constantly evolving trail
featuring works of art on public display around Newbiggin. In 2014 there
were nearly 60 pieces of art, the most famous being Sean Henry's Couple
sculpture: an 8ft-high artwork sited on a new 200yd-long breakwater in the
middle of the bay.

Once Brewed & Winshields Crags

START Once Brewed National Park Visitor Centre car park, GR NY752668

NEAREST POSTCODE NE47 7AN

DISTANCE 5½ miles (9km)

SUMMARY Moderate

MAP OS Explorer OL43 Hadrian's Wall

WHERE TO EAT AND DRINK There is a small refreshments area in the Visitor Centre shop (open Apr–end Oct); The Twice Brewed Inn, T01434-344534, www.twicebrewedinn.co.uk, is almost adjacent to the Visitor Centre on the B6318

Starting from the car park in the Visitor Centre, the route crosses the high ground to the south of the Wall before swinging north and going over one of the Wall's highest sections, including the trig point on Winshields Crags.

START From the car park go out onto the minor road and turn left onto the B6318. Be careful walking along this road past the Twice Brewed public house. Opposite Vallum Lodge Guest House turn left at the public footpath sign, which goes down a narrow way and opens out through a wooden gate into a field. Keeping the wall to your left, walk down the field to cross a footbridge made of a concrete pipe.

① Make your way diagonally right across and up this field, passing to the left of a ruined building. Beyond the building and further up the field there is a fence line with a ladder stile across it. Go over the stile and continue up the field, heading towards another ruined building with trees in front. Go over a stile set in the wall and look under the stone steps on the far side of the stile to see an oddly placed footpath sign. As you clear the rise over the field you will see a wall in the middle distance; the indistinct path is going into the far right-hand corner of that wall. In the wall junction there is a ladder stile to cross, with a public footpath sign pointing back to Once Brewed (1¼ miles). Turn right on a broad track and walk down to a ladder stile leading out onto a minor road.

② Turn right on the minor road and walk back down to the B6318, passing a caravan site on your right. Cross the B6318 to pick up a footpath on the other side of the road. Follow the path down to the end of the fence and wall line and turn diagonally left to cross the Vallum on a footbridge. Continue on the path up an incline till you reach a wall junction and turn right to climb the steps alongside Hadrian's Wall. Continue along the Wall, passing Winshields Crags trig point at 1,132 feet (345m), the highest point along the Wall.

[3] From here the route descends to Steel Rigg car park on a minor road, where you turn right to walk downhill, crossing the B6318 to return to the car park on the opposite side of the road.

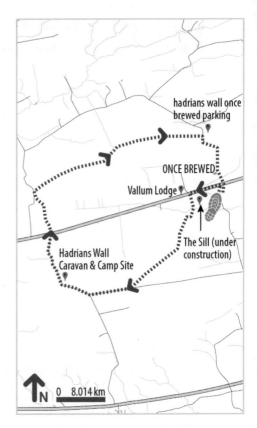

Points of interest

Winshields Crags, at 1,132 feet (345m) on the Ordnance Survey map, is the highest point along the entire length of Hadrian's Wall. It has extensive views to the Cheviots, the Tyne Valley and, on a clear day way over to the west, the Solway.

45 Harthorpe Valley & Middleton Old Town

START Car parking area north of the Carey Burn Bridge, GR NT975249

NEAREST POSTCODE NE71 6RE

DISTANCE 5½ miles (9km)

SUMMARY Moderate

MAP OS Explorer OL16 The Cheviot Hills

WHERE TO EAT AND DRINK There are various cafés and pubs in Wooler

A climb of Brands Hill with views along the Harthope Valley, then easy walking down into Middleton Old Town and a return with views down into Happy Valley.

START Turn right from the parking area, walk down the minor road, cross the Carey Burn Bridge and continue along the road for 1½ miles until you reach the farm at Langlee. Turn left over the metal bridge and then left again, passing a public footpath sign to Old Middleton (2 miles). Continue on the path as it contours up the hillside. You will come to a marker post at a cross track, but continue straight ahead towards a stile on a fence line. Cross the stile and follow the path downhill towards the sheep pens. There is a ladder stile to go over at the sheep pens and the path continues downhill, with the fence line to your right. As you walk down the hillside there is a wall that comes from the left; go over another stile and, keeping the wall to your left, continue downhill to Middleton Old Town.

1 At Middleton Old Town as you pass the last broken down wall, turn left to walk into an old field system. Walk across the field to exit over the fallen stones of the wall and continue ahead to a stile. Go over the stile and continue on the path, keeping the valley to your right-hand side. As the valley disappears behind the wood line the path becomes more of a track and swings down to the left, passing a large pond with old bird hides on your left-hand side.

2 When you have passed the pond, the track will swing away to the right. Leave the track at this point and climb the rise to your left to pick up the clearer path at the top. As you clear the rise you will see the Carey

Burn Valley and the road ahead of you. Continue straight ahead, passing a marker post indicating a path to your left, but ignore this and continue ahead. The path starts to drop down towards the valley and enters the tree line before swinging round to a footbridge, which you cross. Go out onto the road and turn right to get back to the parking area.

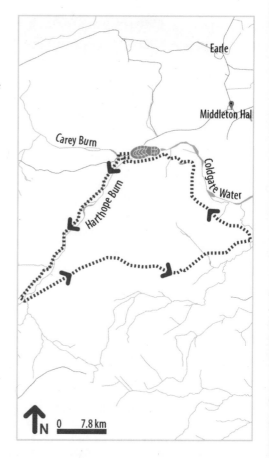

Points of interest

Middleton Old Town: There is documentary evidence that this medieval village existed as far back as 1242, with at least six buildings in the main village facing each other across a wide space. There were eight taxpayers living there in 1296 and 11 tenants in 1580. It is not known for certain when it was finally abandoned, but an old shepherd's cottage shows evidence of occupation until at least the twentieth century.

START Car park near Glendale Tea Room and Garden Centre, Wooler, GR NT994279

NEAREST POSTCODE NE71 6QD

DISTANCE 5½ miles (9km)

SUMMARY Moderate. A walk across the moors to the east of Wooler and the Cheviots

MAP OS Explorer 340 Holy Island & Bamburgh

WHERE TO EAT AND DRINK There are various cafés and pubs in Wooler

A nice easy climb to the top of Weetwood Moor with some great views of the surrounding countryside, including the range of Cheviot Hills.

START From the parking area walk back to the minor road and turn left. You are on part of St Cuthbert's Way as it heads north-east on the last 18 miles to Holy Island. Continue along the road, going uphill, and as the road swings right take the waymarked track with the St Cuthbert's Way sign on your left.

[1] When you reach the top of the hill there is a Y-junction. The left-hand path is a continuation of St Cuthbert's Way; ignore this and take the right-hand path. As you clear the brow of the hill and look ahead, the perspective and distance make it look like there are three woods ahead of you. Stay on the path that is leading towards the right-hand corner of the middle wood. There are other paths crossing the moor but continue on the sometimes indistinct path, passing an old marker sign along the way.

[2] As you approach the wood you will come to a small ditch. At this point if you look to your right you will see a stile crossing the fence line. You need to make your way to the stile, cross it and continue on the path going diagonally left. The path leads to a gate, which you go through, and then follow the path with the white marker posts down to the minor road. Here, there is a public footpath sign pointing back to Weetwood

Moor (½ mile) and Wooler (2¼ miles).

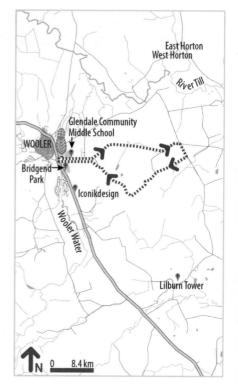

③ Turn left on the minor road and walk down to the crossroads, where you take another minor road to your right. Walk down this road until you come to the farm buildings at Fowberry Mains. Turn right and follow the path with a wall to your left, going through several gates until the path leads onto a track that makes its way to the farm at Fowberry Moor. Follow the track to the right of the houses and then left as it turns behind the barns.

④ The track then turns right and after going through a gate continues straight across the field, where there is another gate. After going through the gate you will come to a T-junction where there is a metal gate in front of you; turn right here and follow the well-defined track. This track turns into a tarmac road just before the entrance to the Radio Station on your right. Continue on the tarmac road until it bends to the right, where there is a public footpath sign pointing diagonally left across the field. Turn left onto the public footpath and where the path rejoins the road follow it downhill to return to the parking area.

Points of interest

After following the white marker posts and as you come out onto the minor road off to the left at approximately GR 023282, there are a number of rocks with cup and ring markings that are the best preserved of any in the surrounding area.

47 Walltown to Once Brewed

START The parking area at
GR NY674661

MAP OS Explorer OL43 Hadrian's
Wall

NEAREST POSTCODE CA8 7HF

DISTANCE 6 miles (9.7km)

SUMMARY Hard; this walk is an
extension of the Walltown to the
Milecastle Inn walk (see above)

WHERE TO EAT AND DRINK There
is a small refreshments area in
the Visitor Centre shop at Once
Brewed (open April–end Oct);
The Twice Brewed Inn is almost
adjacent to the Visitor Centre on
the B6318, To1434-344534,
www.twicebrewedinn.co.uk

One of the best sections of Hadrian's Wall, with great views on a fine day.
The walk ends at the National Park Centre at Once Brewed where a bus, the
AD122, will take you back to Walltown. The bus operates daily between the
end of May and the end of August and a timetable can usually be obtained
from http://www.visithadrianswall.co.uk/.

START From the car park walk diagonally uphill to the right to reach
Walltown Crags, turn right and follow the path as it descends to
cross a stile and climb the steps to regain the height on the other
side of the pass. The path continues along the top, rising and falling
as it follows the contours of the ridge line. After passing through
a wood you will pass the farm at Cockmount Hill and beyond you
will see the outline of Aesica Roman Fort, whose modern name is
Great Chesters.

[1] After looking round the site of the fort cross the ladder stile
over the wall and continue to follow the wall line down the field past
Burnhead to cross the wall over a stile. Cross the road bridge and turn
left into Cawfields Quarry. Walk on the path past the quarry lake,
turning left through a gate and past Milecastle 42. Continue along the
wall until it drops down to a minor road at Caw Gap. Go through the
gate, cross the road, go through the gate opposite and climb the steps
alongside Hadrian's Wall. Continue along the Wall, passing Winshields
Crags trig point at 1,132ft (345m), the highest point along the Wall.

② From here the route descends to Steel Rigg car park on a minor road, where you turn right to walk downhill, crossing the B6318 to reach Once Brewed National Park Visitor Centre on the opposite side of the road.

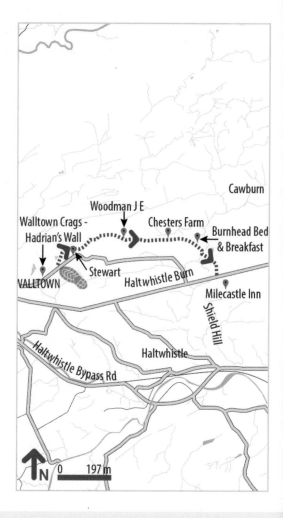

Cawburn

Woodman J E

Walltown Crags - Hadrian's Wall

Chesters Farm

Burnhead Bed & Breakfast

Stewart

WALLTOWN

Haltwhistle Burn

Milecastle Inn

Shield Hill

Haltwhistle Bypass Rd

Haltwhistle

N 0 197 m

Points of interest

Winshields Crags, at 1,132ft (345m) on the Ordnance Survey map, is the highest point along the entire length of Hadrian's Wall. It has extensive views to the Cheviots, the Tyne Valley and, on a clear day way over to the west, the Solway.

Allen Banks & Staward Peel

Start Allen Banks car park, GR NY798640

Nearest postcode NE47 7BP

Distance 6 miles (9.7km)

Summary Moderate; through woodland and river paths, climbing to a thirteenth-century peel tower

Map OS Explorer OL43 Hadrian's Wall

Where to eat and drink The closest town for refreshments is at Haydon Bridge

Start From the car park walk along the path heading into the woods and take the main track beside the River Allen. Continue walking past the newly repaired suspension bridge and continue on the main path beside the river. As you continue on the path you walk out of Allen Banks and into Briarwood Banks, which is one of the few remaining ancient woodlands in Northumberland. Cross the small footbridge with iron railings and then cross the main footbridge over the river.

① Turn right alongside the river and go through the gate that is ahead of you. There is a public footpath sign indicating Staward Peel in 1 mile and the Cupola Bridge in 2½ miles. Follow the path close to the river and as you approach the tree line there is a gate and stile on your left-hand side. Go through the gate onto a track, turning right, which gradually narrows and climbs to higher ground. Shortly after crossing a small footbridge, the track divides. The left-hand track takes a direct route to Staward Peel; it is the first of two steep sections of this walk. There are log-supported steps before giving way to a rocky section of track. Eventually the remains of the Peel come into view and as you continue along the track with steeply sloping sides both left and right, you will come to an information board.

② Keep to the left-hand path, crossing a stile to emerge into an open field. Continue over the field and as the wood line gets closer on your left look for a gate with markers and a stile to the left of the gate. Go over the stile and down the hillside to cross a bridge over a stream. From the bridge the track climbs the second steep section of the walk, where you cross a stile and then head across the field to the corner of a hedge line and follow the hedge line as it clears the top of the field and heads down to a ladder stile next to Harsondale Farm. Turn right on the farm track and then shortly after go over a stile on your left. Follow the track as it passes over several stiles and heads downhill to Sillywrea. The track goes between the farm buildings of Sillywrea, where you turn right and then left at the entrance to the farmhouse.

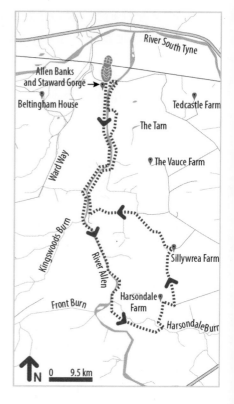

3   Continue on this track, going through several gates and stiles and always keeping the wall or fence line on your right. Depending on the time of year, you may see one of the last remaining farmers who still plough their fields using a horse and plough.

The track will bring you out on a minor road next to Lanefoot House, where you turn left to walk along the lane. As the lane descends and just before it curves sharply left downhill, take the track on your right that is indicated with post and marker.

4   Continue past a ruin and through the gate on your left to where you can continue along a track beside the river. Keep to the main path as it rises to higher ground, ignoring the paths that head closer to the river. These paths take you to the suspension bridge that you passed earlier on. As the main path descends it passes to the right of an open field, at the end of which you turn left into it through a gate, turning right at the bottom back beside the river. As the road bridge comes into view, go under it then over it via a gate on your right and walk down the road, turning left back into the car park.

49 Bolham Lake & Shaftoe Crags

START Boathouse Wood car park, GR NZ083820

NEAREST POSTCODE NE20 0HE

DISTANCE 6 miles (9.7km)

SUMMARY Easy; generally level apart from a short climb

MAP OS Explorer OL42 Kielder Water & Forest

WHERE TO EAT AND DRINK There is a café and visitor information centre in the Boathouse Wood car park (open 10.30am–4.30pm weekends, Bank Holidays and school holidays Easter–Nov; Dec–Easter open from 10.30am but closes earlier at weekends and during school holidays)

PARKING Boathouse Wood, Low House Wood and West Wood. All car parks are in the confines of Bolam Lake (parking charges apply). In summer the main car park at Boathouse Wood is often full. However, there is usually parking available at the other two car parks. This route starts from the Boathouse Wood car park, but it is very easy to pick up from the other two car parks

START From the car park head towards the lake and pick up the path that goes between the lake and the road. As you walk down this path you come to the second car park, Low House Wood. Go out of the car park onto the road and turn right, continuing on the road a short way to meet a road junction. Go straight over the junction and pass a house on your right called Bolam Low House. The third car park, West Wood, is along the road to your right. If you are using this car park you would walk down the path between the wood and the road to arrive at the junction.

1 Just past Bolam Low House on the right-hand side is a stile; cross the stile and continue diagonally across the fields, heading towards a wood. At the entrance to the wood go over a stile and follow the path through the wood and then across the smaller of the two bridges. Turn left on the track and at the T-junction turn right through a gate and

over the stream. There is a footbridge here but it is difficult to cross in the summer because of foliage.

② Go diagonally left across the field to pick up the track that curves round and to the front of Sandyford. Walk along this track past the cottage at West Tofthill and look for a finger-post on your left pointing right towards East Shaftoe Hall. Turn right here and walk over the fields to the track in front of the hall, where you will turn left and continue to a gate leading into Shaftoe Crags. As you walk along the track, look out to the left to see the Devil's Punchbowl. Follow the track as it curves to the right and at the house called Shaftoe Grange take the minor footpath that continues past the building, keeping the boundary wall on your left, and you will come to the track called Salter's Nick.

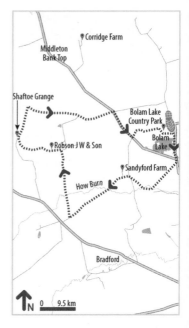

③ Follow the track up the incline through Salter's Nick, keeping the boundary wall to your left, pass through a gate, and continue to the crossroads where you turn right to walk down the minor road. When you reach a road on your right signed for Harnham, on the opposite side of the road is an access gate for Bolam Lakes. Go through the gate and turn right on the path to reach West Wood car park; continue along the path to return to either of the other car parks.

Points of interest

Devil's Punchbowl: The rock gets its name from the fact that at the time of the wedding of Sir Walter Blackett of Wallington Hall, in 1775, the 'Punchbowl' was allegedly filled with wine – its capacity is several gallons!

Salter's Nick: This track was probably used for smuggling illicit salt into Scotland on pack horses during the time of the Salt Tax. The return cargo was often illegally distilled whisky.

Cambo & Kirkwhelpington

START Car park next to Cambo
County First School, GR NZ024859

NEAREST POSTCODE NE61 4BE

DISTANCE 6 miles (9.7km)

SUMMARY Easy; a few slopes, but no
real uphill work

MAP OS Explorer OL42 Kielder
Water & Forest

WHERE TO EAT AND DRINK Dyke Neuk
Inn on the B6343 road,
http://thedykeneuk.co.uk

Apart from a single stretch of road after leaving Elf Hills farm, this walk is along footpaths that cut across Northumberland farmland and through farms that have been used for centuries.

START From the car park turn left on the B6342 and left again at the T-junction signed to the cemetery. Continue past the cemetery, go through the gate and follow the path across the field to another gate in the corner, and then head towards the farm of Elf Hills. Go through the gate just before the farm and then turn right along a track going away from the farm. The track turns into a farm road and leads to a T-junction, where you turn left.

① Continue on the road until you reach the farm road entrance to Fawns, where you turn left and continue to the farm at Fawns. As you pass through the gate at Fawns turn half-right and head across the field in the direction of the gate. Go through the gate and head downhill, with the fence line to your right. Go through another gate at the bottom of the field, where you turn left and continue with the stream on your left. After the stream disappears through the fence you will come to another gate on your left, which you go through. Follow the track down and across the stream, where you join a minor road.

② Turn left on the road away from the village of Kirkwhelpington, and after passing a sign with the word 'Gates' look for a stile on your left with a public footpath sign indicating Broom House (1 mile). The path climbs a hill parallel to the road, where you go over another stile.

Beyond this stile, walk in line with two large trees that you can see ahead and go over a ladder stile in the top corner of the field. Go over a second ladder stile and continue ahead to reach Broom House Farm.

3   Go through the gate into the farmyard and then straight through the metal gate that you can see at the end of the farm buildings. A public footpath sign indicates Cambo (¾ mile), pointing half-left across the field. Go through a gate at the top left of the field and follow the path over a couple of wall stiles as you cut through a wood. Head half-left across the field to a gate in the corner of the field and walk across the next field to exit onto the B6342.

4   Turn left and walk along the road to the minor road on your right, which leads through Cambo village. Turn left past the church, which is worth a visit, left again on the B6343, then right to walk back to the car park.

Points of interest

Ridge and furrow: You cannot but notice as you walk along this route the corrugated appearance of the land. Almost every field has evidence of the old farming practice of ridge and furrow, where over centuries men, horses and oxen would plough the land and harvest the crops each year. Although this type of farming had been going on for generations, it expanded in the eighteenth and nineteenth centuries as grain crops were cultivated to feed the growing populations in the cities. Much of the grain from this part of Northumberland was transported each autumn to the grain port of Alnmouth. The road heading east to the coast became known as the Corn Road.

51 Haltwhistle & Park Village

START Road lay-by, Haltwhistle,
GR NY707638

NEAREST POSTCODE NE49 0HH

DISTANCE 6 miles (9.7km)

SUMMARY Moderate. A walk from
Haltwhistle along the River South
Tyne and through the National Trust-
owned Bellister Estate, passing
through the village of Park, which
was once owned by the Estate

MAP OS Explorer OL43 Hadrian's
Wall

WHERE TO EAT AND DRINK There are
various cafés, pubs and shops in
Haltwhistle

START From the lay-by go west along the road and through the railway
arch on the south side of the road. Go over the bridge and turn right on
the road, bearing right under the A69. After going under the A69, turn
right onto the public footpath indicating Bellister Bank (½ mile). The
footpath leads alongside the river, then turns away up some steps where
there is another public footpath sign to Park Village (¾ mile).

1   Continue on the footpath on the high bank looking down on
the river, but ignore the finger-post on the left indicating Park Village.
Continue on, following the National Trust markers that lead into a wood
and past a caravan site that is down on the right-hand side. The path
comes out on a minor road, where you turn right and cross a bridge over
Park Burn. Just before the weir turn left on a public footpath indicating
Park Village (½ mile). Follow the path up the bank, over a footbridge and
up the steps onto the minor road. Turn right on the road and right again at
the T-junction into Park village. Follow the road as it swings left through
the village, then back out onto the minor road, where you turn right.

2   Walk down the road for a short way and look for a public footpath
sign on your left that indicates Broom House Common and a public
bridleway to Lynnshield (¾ mile). Follow the farm track until you come
to a broken wall on your left, where there are yellow markers indicating

a left turn. Turn left and follow the track down to a gate; go through the gate and continue across the fields through several gates and following a tree-lined path. The path will start to swing right and come close to the old railway line.

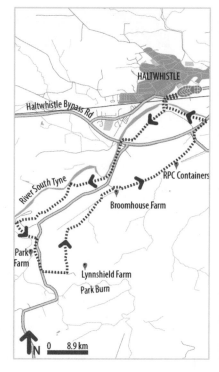

3 The path leads down to the left and over a small bridge, where you turn left and walk down into the corner of the field and over a ladder stile to cross the bridge over the railway. Follow the track past Broomhouse and keep on it as it curves right past another rail bridge and descends down to a gate and onto the railway path. Continue on the path until it comes out on the Plenmeller Rd, where you turn left. Just before the T-junction with the A69, turn right on a well-made track that leads down to the river and then left under the A69 road bridge.

4 On the other side of the A69 one option is to continue on the path back to the bridge that you crossed on leaving Haltwhistle, while the other option is to turn back on yourself and pick up the permissive path that leads up onto the viaduct over the river. Both options will bring you back through the railway arch, where you turn right towards the lay-by.

Points of interest

Park village: Much of the village was once owned by the Bellister Estate, a large area of land on the south side of the River South Tyne. The Bellister Estate and Castle went through a number of owners since first being established in the thirteenth century before the last owners, the Jackson family, presented it to the National Trust in 1975.

Ingram & Old Fawdon Hill

Sᴛᴀʀᴛ Ingram Visitor Centre car park, GR NU017163

Nᴇᴀʀᴇsᴛ ᴘᴏsᴛᴄᴏᴅᴇ NE66 4LT

Dɪsᴛᴀɴᴄᴇ 6 miles (9.7km); 7 miles (11km) using alternative routes

Sᴜᴍᴍᴀʀʏ Moderate

Mᴀᴘ OS Explorer OL16 The Cheviot Hills and OS Explorer 332 Alnwick & Amble

Wʜᴇʀᴇ ᴛᴏ ᴇᴀᴛ ᴀɴᴅ ᴅʀɪɴᴋ Plough Inn, Powburn, T01665-578769; Queens Head, Glanton, T01665-578324; Poachers Rest, Hedgeley Services, T01665-578664

Sᴛᴀʀᴛ From the car park go left on the road past the telephone box, left again at the T-junction and, where the road bears left again, turn right and go through the gate onto a track. There is a finger-post indicating Prendwick (2¼ miles). Walk up the track as it goes steadily uphill, passing to the right of the Iron Age settlement on the summit of Wether Hill.

1 As the track descends and before the gate and stile there is permissive path on the left-hand side with a sign low down on the ground. Turn left and walk down a short cutting, bearing left at the rocks to pass through a gate in the fence. Climb the indistinct path to the gate and fence line. This path is difficult to see and navigate in summer as it tends to get overgrown with bracken.

2 If you miss the permissive path, go over the stile and continue on the track until you are level with the end of the wood to your left. Turn left here and walk on a track to the wood, where you go through a gate and turn left through another gate to walk on a footpath heading uphill to and through the gate in the fence line ahead of you.

3 Having gone either way, both come together at the base of Old Fawdon Hill by the gate. Follow the path as it starts to go behind Old Fawdon Hill; there is a marker post that indicates a route to the left, but ignore this and continue straight on. It is an easy contour around the hill and the path will gradually pull away from the fence line on your right to come close to the wood and an old shed. As you move past the wood the path widens out to a wide track heading towards a wood.

④ Just after the wood on the right-hand side there is a stile over the fence. Go over the stile and continue diagonally down the field to pass through one gate, heading towards the hedge line in front of you.

⑤ In summer it is difficult to see the stile after the wood because of high bracken. An alternative route is to carry on along the track as it curves left then right to reach a gate. Go through the gate and then turn right to contour round below the small hill on your left. Go through another gate and walk downhill to meet the same hedge line.

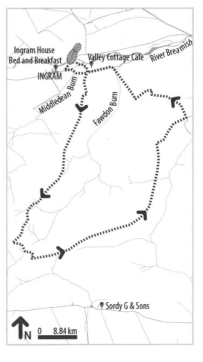

⑥ In the hedge line are two gates; go through the left-hand gate and follow the path beside the hedge line. Continue along the path as the hedge turns right and walk across the field, passing through two gates to come out in the farmyard at Fawdon. Turn left through a gate and follow the track uphill, ignoring the track to the right that goes to Brandon. Once at the crest of the hill you can see Ingram down below. Keep on the track, taking the first left turn, continuing down the hill and turning right at the bottom and then through a gate onto a lane.

⑦ Walk down the lane, through a final gate and turn right to walk down past St Michael and All Angels Church. On the left-hand side there is a track that leads through a wood back into the rear of the main car park.

Points of interest

Hill forts are a feature of the Cheviots. On this relatively short walk there are six forts visible and even more just a short distance away. The Breamish Valley was a very busy area many years ago.

53 Stannington Circular

START **Stannington Village Hall car park, GR NZ214794**

NEAREST POSTCODE **NE61 6EL**

DISTANCE **6 miles (9.7km)**

SUMMARY **Easy**

MAP **OS Explorer 316 Newcastle upon Tyne**

WHERE TO EAT AND DRINK **Ridley Arms, Stannington, www. ridleyarmsstannington.co.uk; Northumberland Cheese Company, Cheese Loft Café, www. northumberlandcheese.co.uk/tea-room (open Mon–Sun, 10am–5pm)**

An easy walk through the woods and fields of the Blagdon Estate, crossing the sixteenth-century Bellasis Bridge and with a possible visit to the Northumberland Cheese Company on the way.

START From the car park turn left past the Ridley Arms pub, following the road as it curves around the crescent, and after crossing the mini-roundabout take the road ahead. Follow this road as it curves to the left, looking out for a public footpath sign on the right indicating Bellasis Bridge (2½ miles). Follow this path through the woods, across a footbridge and then right out of the woods to follow a fence line on your right.

1 Continue along the path, heading straight across the field towards the fence line that you can see in front of you. Turn left when you reach the fence line and continue with this fence line to your right. Cross a stile to enter the edge of a wood and follow the path between the wood and the hedge. The path bears to the left and emerges at a T-junction, where you turn right. To the left is a private road. Follow this track between two fields and then through a wood until it joins a minor road. Continue straight on to the T-junction, where Bellasis Farm Cottage is directly ahead.

2 Bear right on the track past the cottage; it indicates that it is a private road but this is part of the permissive paths that form Blagdon

Estate. Just past the wood turn left over the stile and continue on the path that runs beside the wood on the left-hand side. Follow this path as it reaches the end of the wood and turns right between two fields, coming out on the road at Bellasis Bridge.

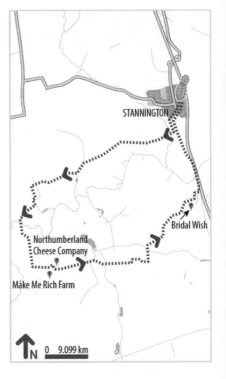

③ Go over the bridge and walk down the road until the off-set crossroads, where you turn left. There is a permitted footpath sign that indicates Bog House (1 mile) and a sign to 'Make Me Rich', which is the location for the Northumberland Cheese Company Farm. Bear left for the Cheese Farm, ignoring the track ahead that just leads to a farm.

④ After leaving the Cheese Farm follow the track away from the farm and towards Bog House, where you bear left past the farm buildings to emerge on the farm road. Continue on the farm road, turning left at the T-junction. Continue straight on, passing a private road to your right, and at the next T-junction turn right. As you walk along the next stretch of minor road, look out for a public footpath sign on the left indicating New Kennels (¾ mile). Turn left on this track and after a short distance look for a path on the left that leads to the edge of the woods.

⑤ Turn right at the wood edge and follow the path down to a track to the houses at New Kennels. Continue on the estate road as it bears left and then right to come out on the main A1, which is heading north. Turn left here and follow the footpath beside the A1, crossing the bridge over the River Blyth. Just after the bridge turn left on an old road that leads away from the A1. This road will pass the public footpath sign to Bellasis Bridge that you took on the way out of Stannington. Continue on to cross the mini-roundabout, heading back to the car park.

54 The Rothbury Terraces

START Cowhaugh car park, Rothbury, GR NU057015

NEAREST POSTCODE NE65 7RW

DISTANCE 6 miles (9.7km)

SUMMARY Moderate

MAP OS Explorer 332 Alnwick & Amble

WHERE TO EAT AND DRINK The closest town for refreshments is Rothbury

A short climb out of Rothbury onto the carriageways of the Cragside Estate, with extensive views over to the Simonside Hills and, further away, the Cheviots.

START From the car park cross the footbridge over the River Coquet and make your way through the lane to the main road through Rothbury. Cross to the far side of the road, turn right and walk past the shops until you reach the Queens Head pub. Turn left here and follow Brewery La as it swings to the right past Addycombe Cottages. Opposite the end of the cottages on the left-hand side is a short section of road leading to a footpath that will take you uphill onto Hillside Rd.

[1] Turn right on the road and walk just past the distinctive detached house called High House to turn left up a signed footpath. Continue along the footpath until you reach an off-set crossing of tracks; turn right and immediately left to pick up an overgrown waymarked path heading uphill. This path ends at a T-junction, with a well-maintained track running on the edge of the woods above Rothbury.

[2] Turn left on the track and continue along it until you go through a gate that leads out onto the moors. Just after the gate look out for a finger-post on the right, pointing across the moors in the direction a wood. Turn right here and follow the track across the moors until you reach the wood. Go through a gate and turn right on a path running on the edge of the wood past some distinctive groups of beech trees on your right.

[3] At the main T-junction turn left on the track until you reach a

gate. Go straight ahead through the gate, ignoring the tracks on your left and right. The track will take you up an incline and will swing around to the left before heading downhill through a gate and then alongside a wood on your left-hand side. Look out for the entrance to Blue Mill Wood on your left-hand side and take this track leading through the wood.

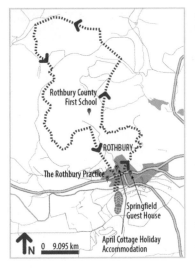

4   As the track goes through the wood it starts to loop round to the left as a wall appears on your right. Turn right, keeping the wall on your right to cross over a wall stile. Follow the footpath, crossing over one path, until you reach a main sandy track where you turn right. Stay on this track as it curves left and right to bring you back round towards Rothbury. Keep on the track past the TV transmitter masts on your right and you will see the gate ahead of you that led you out of the woods above Rothbury. Just before the gate a marker post indicates a footpath on your right. Turn right and follow the path as it heads downhill into Rothbury. The first part is across moorland and then down through woodland before coming out on a minor road.

5   Follow the road downhill until it comes to an off-set T-junction; to the right the path continues downhill. At the T-junction with a lane turn left and look for the undertaker's premises on your right. The path leads down from here and comes out onto the main road in Rothbury. Cross the road to pick up the lane that will lead you back over the bridge to the car park.

Points of interest

Cragside House on the outskirts of Rothbury was built over the period 1870–85. During the building a lot of work was carried out in the grounds of the house, including the construction of the carriageways that gave Lord Armstrong and his family the chance to tour the estate in a horse and carriage. This walk covers some of the original route of the carriageway.

55 Walltown & the Tipalt Burn

START Small parking area alongside the road, GR NY674661

NEAREST POSTCODE CA8 7HF

DISTANCE 6 miles (9.7km)

SUMMARY Moderate

MAP OS Explorer OL43 Hadrian's Wall

WHERE TO EAT AND DRINK There is a shop at Walltown Quarry Visitor Centre and a café at the Roman Army Museum

Starting from the parking area close to Walltown Quarry Visitor Centre, the walk includes a section of Hadrian's Wall, Walltown Quarry and scenic countryside south of the Wall. The route passes the remains of Thirlwall Castle and the drift mine at Wrytree.

START From the parking area walk uphill and turn left to follow Hadrian's Wall. The Wall comes to an end overlooking Walltown Quarry. Turn left and follow the path down the hillside to pass through a gate on the right and continue the descent into the quarry. Keep on the main path. At the Y-junction bear right and at the next Y-junction bear left to arrive at Walltown Quarry Visitor Centre.

1 Cross the car park, exit through a gate and walk along a path to a T-junction where you turn left. The path will exit through a gate onto the road; cross the road and pass through another gate on the opposite side of the road. Walk down the grassy path, crossing a ladder stile, and follow the track over a footbridge. To your left is a gate that you go through to walk on the Pennine Way a short distance. Take the opportunity to visit Thirlwall Castle, which is just ahead.

2 After visiting the castle follow the Pennine Way alongside the Tipalt Burn as far as the railway line. Turn left through a gate to follow a footpath between the railway and the burn into Greenhead. When the path exits onto the road, turn left over the bridge and then right on the footpath signed to College. Follow the path past the old vicarage and across the fields to College Farm. As you approach the farm, head slightly left to exit onto the farm road through a gate.

3   Turn left and uphill towards Wrytree Farm. As you walk up the farm road look out for a stile on your left, which you cross, and then a second stile just beyond. These stiles lead you around the back of the farm and you exit onto a track through a gate. Turn left on the track and walk past the old colliery of Wrytree Drift until you come to a Y-junction with a track leading back on your right. Turn onto the track, go under the electricity cables and then turn left to follow an indistinct path parallel to the electricity pylon. The path comes close to a wall on your right and leads to a ladder stile. Go over the ladder stile, turn right on the minor road and then over another ladder stile on your left-hand side where there is a finger-post indicating Fell End (¼ mile). Cross the field, keeping the wall to your left, and go through a gate. Turn left and, again keeping the wall to your left, walk down to the B6318.

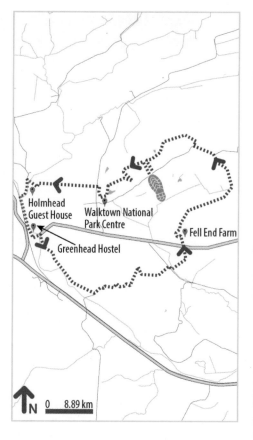

4   Cross the road and take the track leading to Fell End Farm; go round the front of the farm and then to the right of the barn. Follow a rough track that leads away diagonally right from the farm to a gate, which you go through. Cross the next field, picking up a track that leads to another gate and out onto a road. Turn left, heading for Walltown Farm. Just before the farm turn right on a track and follow a path up the rising ground to reach Hadrian's Wall. Turn left and follow the wall on the high ground until you can see your car down the slope to your left.

START Wylam car park, GR NZ118646

POSTCODE NE41 8EE

DISTANCE 6 miles (9.7km)

SUMMARY Easy; riverside paths, woodland tracks, undulating farmland and minor roads

MAP OS Explorer 316 Newcastle upon Tyne

WHERE TO EAT AND DRINK Boathouse Inn, Wylam, T01661-853431; Fox and Hounds, Wylam, T01661-853256; The Boathouse, Newburn, T0191-2290326

An easy walk along both sides of the River Tyne between Wylam and Newburn.

START The car park in Wylam is just behind the war memorial; from the back of the car park there is a main track, which forms part of the National Cycle Network Route 72. This track was once a railway line called the North Wylam Loop, and North Wylam Station is now the car park. If you look closely you can see the edge stones of one of the platforms on the far side of the track. Turn right onto this track and keep walking past the National Trust sign for George Stephenson's birthplace (½ mile).

① Once you have reached the cottage where George Stephenson was born (it contains a museum and tea rooms) turn right and head down to the river, where you can go through a gate and continue on a narrower path beside the river. Keep on this path, avoiding the temptation to head back left where you can rejoin the main track at various places. The church spire that you can see on the other side of the river is the thirteenth-century Holy Cross Church of Ryton.

② Eventually the path will join the main cycle route, with a sign indicating Newburn (1 mile); here you enter the Tyne Riverside Country Park. Walk past the playground and the fitness apparatus and you will approach the car park; the Visitor Centre is to your right but is only open during the summer months. It's worth taking a moment to read the display boards in the car park that describe the Battle of Newburn Ford in 1640 between the Scottish army and the English army of Charles I. The English Civil War has its beginnings in this battle.

3 Leave the car park, cross a wooden bridge and continue on the track heading for Newburn Bridge, which you can see ahead. Before crossing the bridge, take a moment to look at the flood markers on the wall beneath the Boathouse pub sign; the highest flood marker recorded in 1771 destroyed just about every bridge along the River Tyne.

4 Across the bridge and heading back to Wylam, you pass through Ryton Willows Nature Reserve and the track is called the Keelmans Way. Continue along this track with the train line close to your left-hand side, and as the train line bears away left the track continues beside Ryton golf course.

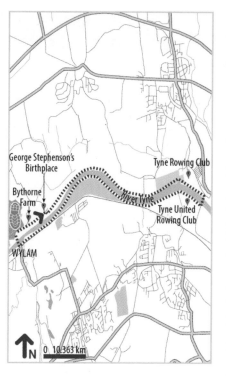

5 Ignore the sign for Clara Vale on your left and continue on with the railway line, coming back in beside the track. The track then turns left and you come to Wylam Station. Walk out through the station car park and cross Wylam Bridge and you will arrive back at the car park behind the war memorial.

Points of interest

George Stephenson's birthplace: On the track leading from Wylam to Newburn, Stephenson was born here on 9 June 1781. Now owned by the National Trust, the cottage is open Mar–Oct Thurs–Sun, and Nov–Feb on weekends.

57 Alnham & the Shepherd's Cairn

Start Church at Alnham, GR NT990109 (park on grass verge close to church)

Postcode NE66 4TL

Distance 6½ miles (10.5km)

Summary Moderate; a walk in a remote area

Map OS Explorer OL16 The Cheviot Hills

This route leads into what feels like quite a remote area that goes along Salter's Road to High Knowes, where the memorial to two shepherds is situated. The route then heads south on a sometimes indistinct path before turning east back to Alnham. There are good views in all directions.

Start Walk along the minor road past the church and Tower House and turn right at the permissive byway sign that indicates Shankhouse (3 miles) and Low Bleakhope (5 miles). After going through a gate just after a wood turn diagonally right towards a marker post on a track. When you reach the track turn left and follow it to a Y-junction, where you take the left-hand path. The path is quite broad here and is part of Salter's Road; continue over the ladder stile and then slightly right on the track.

1   Continue along the track, heading towards a circular sheepfold; when you reach the sheepfold take the left-hand track that is heading uphill. As you get to the top of the hill there is a restricted byway marker, which is where you take the left-hand path. Just beyond is a large marker stone with a path that is also turning left. At the next Y-junction take the right-hand path and continue uphill and you will reach the Shepherds' Cairn at GR 967126.

2   From the memorial keep on the track as it heads downhill to a minor road, cross the road and continue on a path that joins the main path on a T-junction. Looking to your right you can see the finger-post and to your left is a marker. Turn left and follow the path across the fellside on an indistinct path with marker posts until you come to a gate. Go through the gate and head down into the burn. The path leading down into the burn is behind a large rock and you cross above the small

waterfall; the path leads up the other side diagonally left.

③   As you climb the rise there is a marker post in front of you, and beyond there is a stile over a fence. After crossing the stile go past the concrete structure, which is all that remains of Todd Stones farm, and you will see a marker post ahead of you. The path becomes broader, but as it approaches the wood it becomes less clear. Keep to the left of the wood and head towards the strip wood in front of you. The stile that goes through the wood is about 200yds from the right-hand edge of the wood.

④   Go over the stile, through the wood and exit over another stile, where you turn left and head towards a stile over a fence. After a second stile head towards the right-hand edge of the wood in front of you. Go through the wood, using the stile and gate, and head along the ridge downhill towards a farm track. On the other side of the track is a gate and a track beyond, which leads to a footbridge. Once over the footbridge go past the bungalow at Hazeltonrig and turn left up a path that winds up the hillside. At the top of the hill go through the gate and cross two fields. After going through a gate, the path goes downhill and you will see the church down below. When you reach the road, turn right back to the parking area.

Points of interest

Shepherds' Cairn: Located at High Knowes, the cairn is a memorial to two shepherds, John Scott and William Middlemas, who lost their lives close to this spot in a blizzard in November 1962. Because of this tragedy a Search and Rescue team was formed in 1963, which is now known as the Northumberland National Park Mountain Rescue Team.

College Valley & Hethpool Linn

START **Hethpool car park, GR NT893280**

NEAREST POSTCODE **NE71 6TW**

DISTANCE **6½ miles (10.5km)**

SUMMARY **Easy**

MAP **OS Explorer OL16 The Cheviot Hills**

WHERE TO EAT AND DRINK **Cafe Maelmin, Milfield, www.cafemaelmin.co.uk; there are also various cafés and pubs in Wooler**

The College Valley is restricted by permit to 12 cars per day, so there is very little traffic on the first section. The route returns on the east side of the College Burn and follows a footpath until Hethpool Mill. There is a short section on St Cuthbert's Way before the route turns towards the waterfalls of Hethpool Linn and a return to the car park.

START From the parking area walk into the College Valley on the tarmac road. Continue on the road past Whitehall Farm until you reach the Y-junction. Cuddystone Hall is to your left and the war memorial is in front of you. Take the left branch and cross Sutherland Bridge over the College Burn. A short way from the bridge there is an opening on the left with a gate and public footpath sign indicating Hethpool Mill (2 miles). Go through the gate and walk along the grassy track to go through a metal gate.

① Just before the next metal gate turn left at a marker post and follow the path down through the trees. Cross two small burns and pass through a gate, dropping down through some more trees to walk close beside the College Burn. The path makes its way through the gorse bushes and comes to a gate, which you go through. Bear to your left and climb the grassy bank, keeping the fence line to your left.

② At the top of the bank go through a wooden gate to pass through a new plantation of trees. Look to your left for the path dropping down the bankside, follow it down and continue through newly planted trees. Go past Hethpool Mill on your right and, as the track bends to the left to go over the bridge, continue on the stony track up the hillside. You are now on a section of St Cuthbert's Way.

3. Continue along the track through another new plantation, go through an opening in the fence to turn sharp left through a tall wooden gate, and follow the path in front of you. St Cuthbert's Way turns away to your right, but continue straight on with the fence line on your left. Go over the stile to your left and then over the footbridge on your right. This is Hethpool Linn and, depending on the time of year and the density of the trees and vegetation, you may be able to see the waterfalls.

4. After the footbridge turn left to cross a small footbridge and then a stile, which is to your right. The path goes over a section of boardwalk and through a gate and heads across the field towards a stile. Go over the stile and walk up towards the road leading from the bridge near Hethpool Mill. Turn left on the minor road and walk back to the car park.

College Burn

Hethpool house
Bed & Breakfast

Hethpool Lake

N 0 9.38 km

59 Corbridge & Aydon Castle

START **Corbridge free car park,**
GR NY988640

NEAREST POSTCODE **NE45 5AU**

DISTANCE **6½ miles (10.5km)**

SUMMARY **Moderate**

MAPS **OS Explorer OL43 Hadrian's
Wall and OS Explorer 316 Newcastle
upon Tyne**

WHERE TO EAT AND DRINK **There are
various cafés, pubs and shops in
Corbridge**

The route goes east out of Corbridge on a minor road before heading north
over the A69 to visit Aydon Castle, before dropping and returning south
back over the A69 into Corbridge. There are good views over the Tyne Valley
during the return route.

START From the car park turn left over the bridge and at the T-junction
turn right. There is a pavement on the left-hand side of the road
(B6530), which you follow out of Corbridge until the road starts to
bend to the right. Turn left at the public footpath sign indicating
Thornbrough (¼ mile).

1 As you cross the minor road in Thornbrough, go straight ahead
until you reach the fence line that borders the A69. Turn right and in the
corner is a stile, which will lead along a path to the road bridge crossing
the A69. Turn left and follow this road past Thornbrough Lime Kilns on
your left and the farm just beyond on the right. Before the road bends to
the left, turn left over a ladder stile at a public footpath sign indicating
Aydon Road (¼ mile).

2 Cross the field, heading to your right to go over two stiles, and exit
onto the road, where you turn right. At the road sign for Aydon turn
left and walk down the road past the houses, turning right at a public
footpath sign indicating Aydon Castle (½ mile). Follow the track into the
field and go straight over the small hill to your front. As you approach
the fence line, turn right and follow the fence line as it bends around the
field perimeter. In the corner is a stile, which you go over, and then turn
left down a slope and right to head towards the stream. The footbridge

comes into view, which you cross, and then follow the path up the bankside.

③ Cross the wall stile and turn left at the public bridleway sign that indicates Corbridge (2 miles). Go past Aydon Castle and through a gate, heading back down the bankside to follow a path through the woods and crossing another footbridge on the way. Exit the woods through a gate and go diagonally left across the field. Keep going downhill to pick up a track beside a wood that will lead down to the A69, where you turn left to parallel the A69.

④ Turn right when you reach the road bridge and right again at the public bridleway sign indicating Deadridge Lane (¼ mile). Follow the path as it heads down and to the right of the housing estate. When you reach

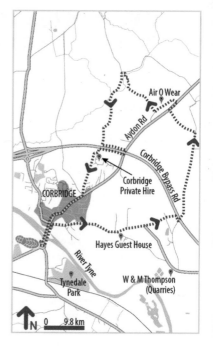

the T-junction turn right along the main road, which will lead you down and over the bridge back to the car park. If you have time, turn right before the bridge to explore the older part of Corbridge.

Points of interest

Aydon Castle: This is a thirteenth-century manor house that has remained almost unaltered over the centuries. It is now an English Heritage site and is open Apr–early Nov.

Corbridge: Originally a Roman supply town, the remains of the Roman site including a museum are open for visits. The village grew in medieval times and has a range of architecture reflecting different styles over the years, including a fine bridge built in 1674 and widened in 1881. The village has various shops, cafés and pubs mostly centered around the market square, with the Saxon church of St Andrew's on one side.

Featherstone Rowfoot & Coanwood

START Car park (South Tyne Trail), GR NY682607

NEAREST POSTCODE NE49 0JG

DISTANCE 6½ miles (10.5km)

SUMMARY Moderate; the walk crosses farmland and moorland

MAP OS Explorer OL43 Hadrian's Wall

WHERE TO EAT AND DRINK There are various cafés, pubs and shops in Haltwhistle

Although the start is on a minor road, the majority of this route uses mostly public footpaths and bridleways, crossing farmland and moorland to reach Coanwood Friends Meeting House.

START From the car park go out onto the road and turn right, continue around the bend and go left at the T-junction. Continue along the road, taking the left-hand bend downhill, and just after the bridge over Park Burn go right over the ladder stile onto the public footpath indicating Broomhouse (1¼ miles) and Lynnshield (½ mile). Go to the end of the field and turn left up the bank and through the gate on the right at the top.

1. Walk alongside the fence line and exit out of the field through a gate onto a farm road. Just before the farm there is a gate on the right, directing you around the side of the farm, and there is also a public footpath sign on the side of a tin shack indicating Broomhouses (1 mile). On the far side of the farm there is a marker post indicating a right turn along the fence line. Follow the fence line to a gate, which you go through, and turn right to follow the path alongside Park Burn and past the waterfall. The path begins to move away from the burn and becomes indistinct as it goes across the grass, but you are generally heading towards Low Ramshaw Farm.

2. Before the farm, start to head uphill towards a lone tree; beyond the tree, climb the bank and you will see a gate ahead of you in the wall line. The path becomes clearer as you approach the gate; go through it and follow the track as it turns to the right to approach Low Ramshaw

Farm. Pass through the small gates in front of the farm and then turn left after the last gate to follow a path downhill and across Park Burn over a footbridge.

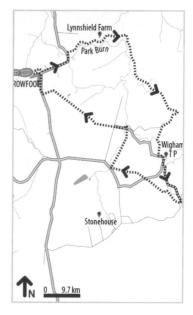

③ Climb the bank and follow the wall line on your left to the track leading through Hargill House, turning right to head down to the minor road, where you turn left. Follow this road until you come to a bridge on your right leading into Burn House and the Coanwood Friends Meeting House.

④ After visiting the small chapel turn right towards the farm, but immediately turn right through a metal gate and head diagonally left across the field. Follow the markers across the fields to exit through a gate onto a minor road. Just to the left on the other side of the road is another gate that will take you across the fields over ladder stiles, the last one bringing you out onto another minor road.

⑤ Immediately to the right of the ladder stile is a wall stile, which you cross, and then walk across the field next to the stream. The path leads up to and across a bridge on your left next to a mill house. Continue on the track down to the minor road and ahead is a ladder stile, which you go over. Follow the fence line on your right, crossing the stile that you come to, and turn left to head across the field and over a broken-down wall, aiming for a stile that is on the fence line below the stand of trees.

⑥ Cross the stile and head to the right of the trees; at the top of the slope walk diagonally right towards a ladder stile in the corner of the field. Go over the ladder stile and again go diagonally right past the gorse bushes and into the corner of the field, cross a stile, walk down the field and cross a second stile to exit onto a minor road.

⑦ Turn right on the road to walk towards Featherstone Rowfoot. Just before the T-junction there is a track on your left that will lead you back to the car park.

Flodden Battle Site & Pallisburn

START Flodden Field car park,
GR NT888372

NEAREST POSTCODE TD12 4SN

DISTANCE 6½ miles (10.5km)

SUMMARY Moderate

MAP OS Explorer 339 Kelso,
Coldstream & Lower Tweed Valley

WHERE TO EAT AND DRINK The Blue
Bell Inn, Crookham,
www.bluebellcrookham.co.uk

From the car park the route goes round the Flodden battlefield, where there are information boards to explain the battle. Then the route heads north to pass through part of the Pallisburn Estate, before returning to Flodden via St Paul's Church in Branxton.

START Walk up the steps from the car park to start the Battlefield Trail. Turn off to visit the monument and then continue along the field edge. As the trail continues around the site it will exit onto a road leading down the hill back to Branxton. Turn right here and, just before the road swings to the right, turn left through a gate then right along the fence line.

①   Turn left at the field end and walk to the bottom of the field to go through a gate, and continue across the field with a fence line to your right. Cut round the new plantation to the end of the field, go through the gate and turn right. At the end of the field go through a gate and follow the main track until it turns to the right, where there is a stile that leads into a wood. Cross the stile, go through the wood and over the stile at the far end. Turn left and walk downhill to go through the gate and exit onto a minor road.

②   Turn left and walk down to the T-junction and turn right, continue past a cottage and go left over a ladder stile with a public footpath sign indicating Inch Plantation (¼ mile). Go across the field through a gate and pass through the plantation to a stile. Walk up the slope to another stile and bear right round the field edge to exit through a gate onto the A697 and turn right. Walk down the road a short way, turning left on a minor road signed for Crookham Eastfield.

③ Follow the minor road past the farm and turn sharp left between the barns. Go diagonally left across the field; depending on the time of year, you may have to walk round the field edge to meet the gate in the fence line. Again, go diagonally left across the field to go through another gate, where you turn right to follow the tarmac road past Pallinsburn House.

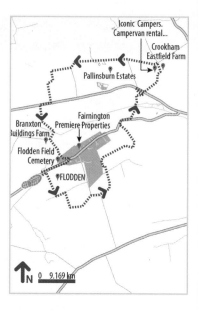

④ At the Y-junction bear left and at the next Y-junction bear right to follow the farm track through the farm at Cookstead and down to the A697. Turn right and walk along the road a short distance to some cottages on your right-hand side, where you cross the road to turn left on a public footpath that indicates Branxton (1 mile).

⑤ Follow the rough path down and to the left; at this point there is a great view of Flodden battlefield in front of you, with the memorial directly ahead on the rising ground. Almost at the end of the field turn right through a gate, cross a footbridge and go over a stile. Walk across the field to another stile that you can see to the left of a cottage. After crossing the stile, turn left up the road and walk towards the church at Branxton.

⑥ The road makes a right-hand turn past the church, and on the left-hand side next to the church car park there is a continuation of the battlefield path that will lead you back to the car park.

Points of interest

🔍 **Flodden battlefield**: The last battle where a ruling monarch was killed on British soil and where perhaps 10,000 men from the Scottish army were killed in just 3 hours. Flodden is a small battlefield which is easily walked, and the views from both sides give a real sense of what happened on 9 September 1513.

Fourstones & Bridge End

START Lay-by north of Fourstones, GR NY888681

NEAREST POSTCODE NE47 5DG

DISTANCE 6½ miles (10.5km)

SUMMARY Moderate

MAP OS Explorer OL43 Hadrian's Wall

WHERE TO EAT AND DRINK The Boatside Inn, Warden, T01434-602233, http://www.theboatsideinn.com; The Railway Inn, Fourstones, T01434-674711

Starting from Fourstones village, the route goes along the River South Tyne to the River North Tyne. It then heads up to Warden church, with the oldest Saxon tower in Northumberland, and on to the Iron Age fort on Warden Hill.

START From the lay-by walk down the road to Fourstones, cross the road and take the minor road downhill, passing the Railway Inn, and cross the Tyne Valley Railway. At the riverside turn left and walk in front of the cottage through a gate and then along the path beside the River South Tyne. Continue along the path, crossing a wall stile.

1 The path will exit onto the road with Fourstones Paper Mill on your right; turn right and walk down the road past the paper mill. When you reach the Boatside Inn look left of the bridge and follow the public footpath sign down and to the left of the cottage to emerge over a short flight of steps on a riverside path. Turn left and follow the path until you reach the junction of the rivers South and North Tyne.

2 You will have to retrace your steps from the river junction; back at the Boatside Inn turn right away from the bridge to pass under the railway line towards the village of Warden. At the village the road bears left away from Warden, but take your time to visit the church that you can see to the right. Continue along the road as it climbs uphill past the gate that leads to High Warden and take the next left turn at a sign for High Warden Thistlerigg Farm. There is also a public bridleway sign indicating Fourstones (1½ miles) and Whinney Hill (1½ miles). Bear left at the sign for Fourstones and at the top of the track turn left and follow the bridleway to Fourstones. At the end of the bridleway go through a

gate and bear left towards a radio mast that is ahead of you.

③   To the left of the radio mast is a gate that you go through, with a public bridleway sign pointing diagonally left across the field towards a wood line. Ignore the sign and walk straight up the field, heading towards another gate with a trig point to its right. Go through the gate. You are now on the Iron Age fort of Warden Hill. Go diagonally left over the fort to exit through an opening in the ditch walls, head straight towards the wood and pass through a gate along a track down through the wood. At the track junction turn right through a gate, passing a finger-post indicating Fourstones (¾ mile) and Whinney Hill (¾ mile).

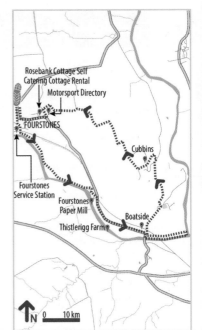

④   At the cottage turn left through another gate and shortly after on the left-hand side of the track is a finger-post pointing the way to Fourstones. Turn left through the gate and then right along an old cart track, through a farmyard and then left along a short stretch of track to reach a road. Turn left and then right at the T-junction to walk down the road into Fourstones. At the small church in Fourstones turn right to walk back to the lay-by.

Points of interest

Fourstones Paper Mill: The mill, founded in 1763, is one of the oldest paper mills in the country.

Warden Church: The church of St Michael and All Angels was consecrated in AD 704 and has the oldest Saxon tower in Northumberland.

Warden Hill: One of the best preserved Iron Age forts in the area.

START Greenleighton Quarry car park, GR NZ034915

NEAREST POSTCODE NE61 4JY

DISTANCE 6½ miles (10.5km)

SUMMARY Moderate; a walk in quite a remote area for much of the time

MAP OS Explorer OL42 Kielder Water & Forest

WHERE TO EAT AND DRINK There is a café and visitor information centre at Fontburn Reservoir, which is open during the summer months. More distant are places in Rothbury and Morpeth

From Greenleighton the route heads towards the Fontburn Reservoir, before heading west on good tracks to skirt the western edge of the reservoir, then south over moorland and fields back to Greenleighton.

START From the car park turn right on the track and walk alongside the old quarry. Continue until you reach a gate beside a water tank to your left. The signs on the gate indicate the Greenleighton walk; the one pointing left is the return route. The one pointing to the right is the route you are going to take.

① Go through the gate and bear right to reach the trig point. Continue on the track with the quarry to your right. As you reach the end of the quarry the track swings to the right and continues across the fields with the reservoir to your left. You will pass two marker posts and go over a footbridge with a wood in front of you. The third marker post is before the wood and indicates a left turn down towards the reservoir.

② At the reservoir go through a gate and turn right; the Greenleighton route diverges here and goes off to the left. Continue on the path, which gets wider as you get further round the reservoir. The path turns left and goes through the car park, with the Visitor Centre to your right. After leaving the car park continue on the access road, which crosses the dam wall, then bear right until you reach a track on your left. Turn left here and continue all the way towards Newbiggin Farm.

③ The track left goes past the farm, but just opposite the farmhouse

is a gate on the left-hand side, which you go
through, followed immediately by another
gate on your right, then walk down the slope
to cross a stile. Continue ahead and you will
reach a finger-post indicating the Waterside
Trail. Follow the sign as the path leads
through a gate and follows the western edge
of the reservoir, crossing a footbridge over
a stream. Continue on the Waterside Trail
until it bears left over a small stream, where
you head right up the slope towards the tall
marker post.

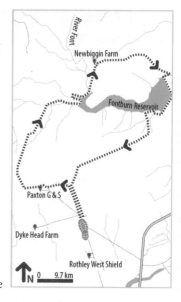

4   At the marker post go straight ahead,
following the track; there is a sign for the
Greenleighton walk but ignore this. Go
through a gate then over a stream and
continue until you meet a cross track, where
you turn left. You are heading towards the gate
that you can now see in front of you, but as
you approach the gate bear right to go through the smaller wooden gate.

5   Continue across the field, heading towards the top right corner,
where you go through a gate and along a track through the wood.
Continue towards Greenleighton Farm. Go past the farm, going straight
ahead with the wall line to your right. As you go further along, the water
tank that you saw at the start of the walk is ahead of you.

6   Walk up to the water tank, turn right through the gate and head
back down the track to the car park.

Points of interest

Fontburn Reservoir: The reservoir was built between 1901 and
1908 to provide fresh water to areas of Tynemouth. To the east of
the reservoir is a 12-span viaduct that use to carry the Scots Gap
to Rothbury railway line 60ft above the River Font. The railway predates the
reservoir by some 30 years; it was completed in 1870. Both structures are
fine examples of engineering carried out in one of the most difficult-to-reach
places in Northumberland.

64 Humbleton & Black Law

Start **Humbleton, GR NT976284**

Nearest postcode **NE71 6SU**

Distance **6½ miles (10.5km)**

Summary **Hard**

Map **OS Explorer OL16 The Cheviot Hills**

Where to eat and drink **There are various cafés and pubs in Wooler**

Parking **On the grass verge at Humbleton**

A walk of two halves – quite hard on the first section but a relatively easy route on the return. Good views over Millfield Plain in the first half and views of the Cheviot Hills on the way back.

Start **Turn left on the stone track leading away from Humbleton and walk uphill until you reach a gate on the right, with a public bridleway sign indicating Gleadscleugh (1½ miles); turn right here. Cross a stile and continue on the bridleway, ignoring a right branching track until you come to a waymarker with the public bridleway pointing off to the right. Follow the bridleway, passing several waymarkers and generally keeping a wall on your right-hand side. Go through a gate at the wall end and continue on over rough pasture. Go through the gate and start to climb the hill; at the top of the hill there is another gate, and the bridleway continues towards Gleadscleugh.**

1 Another gate leads downhill to your right; through one more gate and the bridleway zigzags down and over Akeld Burn to come out on the main track, with Gleadscleugh to your right. Turn left and walk uphill until you come to a small wood on your left-hand side. Go through a gate, turn left and follow the sign for St Cuthbert's Way. At the end of the wood go through a gate and, as the track bears right, turn left on a grassy track. Continue past a large pile of stones, heading towards a gate that you can see ahead on the skyline. When you reach the gate do not go through it, but turn left, keeping to the signs for St Cuthbert's Way.

2 There are several gates or stiles on this section. As you pass Black

Law the track swings to the left and then to the right past Gains Law. As the track descends down the hillside it swings left to join another track. Go through the gate on your left and go straight ahead, ignoring the right turn for St Cuthbert's Way.

3 Continue along this track, passing the public bridleway sign to Gleadscleugh that you took on the way out, and return to Humbleton.

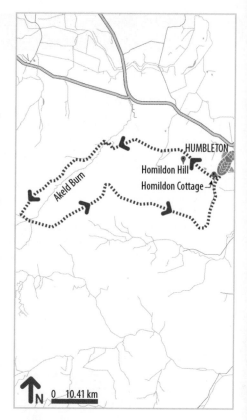

Points of interest

St Cuthbert's Way: This is a 62½-mile-long distance route that is generally walked from Melrose in Scotland to Holy Island in Northumbria. The section of St Cuthbert's Way on this walk is part of the route passing through the Cheviot Hills and emerging at Wooler.

Rothbury & Lordenshaws Hill Fort

START Cowhaugh car park,
GR NU057015

NEAREST POSTCODE NE65 7RW

DISTANCE 6½ miles (10.5km)

SUMMARY Easy

MAP OS Explorer 332 Alnwick &
Amble

WHERE TO EAT AND DRINK The closest
town for refreshments is Rothbury

From Rothbury this walk goes along the River Coquet, before heading south towards the Simonside Hills. After going east along a road at the base of the Simonside Hills, the route heads back to Rothbury passing Lordenshaws Hill Fort and the cup and ring stone markings.

START From the car park cross the footbridge over the River Coquet and turn left to follow the riverside footpath. Walk along the footpath until the river bends away from you and a gate on your left leads across the fields to a very obvious raised footbridge. Cross the footbridge, which was designed this way to prevent it being swept away in floods, and then follow the track, keeping the fence line on your left.

[1] Turn left at the end of the track and follow the minor road as it loops round to the left, ignoring the two roads leading off on your right. Keep on this road for a short distance, looking for a finger-post pointing right at a stile. Go over the stile and continue to cross the field in front of you. As you climb the incline you will meet a fence line; keep the fence line on your left and continue uphill.

[2] As the hill levels out you will pass a marked track on your left, but continue on to go through a gate and then a short section of track through a wood to emerge on a minor road with a cattle crossing on your right. Turn left on the minor road and continue along it until you come to the car park at Lordenshaws. A finger-post at the car park entrance indicates Rothbury in 2 miles.

[3] Turn left through the car park and follow the main track on the

far side of the car park as it heads downhill. Take a moment to detour left to view the cup and ring markings on a large rock, before continuing back on the main path. As you walk downhill look to your right as you pass Lordenshaws Hill Fort. In summer with the bracken it is difficult to see its size but at other times of the year you can still make out the ditches and entrances of this impressive structure.

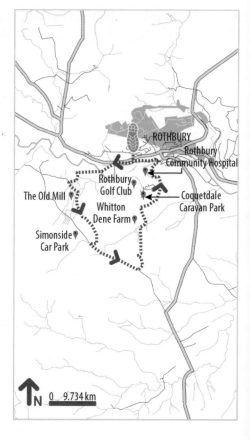

4   Continue downhill and through a gate on your right to pass through Wittondean and then left through another gate to make your way out onto Hillheads Rd. At the T-junction turn right, and further along pass Sharpe's Folly before taking the left-hand turn at the Y-junction. Just after the road has curved to the left, take the road on your right to walk downhill past the hospital and back to the car park.

Points of interest

Cup and ring marks: The marks on the rock at Lordenshaws are Bronze Age and while their significance is unknown it is thought they may have a religious connection or perhaps are a map of other hill forts. They could also indicate the landing sites of flying saucers, but that may be going a bit too far.

66 Rothbury & Wannie Lines

Start National Trust Regional Office car park, GR NZ037864

Nearest postcode NE61 4EG

Distance 6½ miles (10.5km)

Summary Easy; a few slopes but no real uphill work

Map OS Explorer OL42 Kielder Water & Forest

Where to eat and drink Dyke Neuk Inn on the B6343 road, http://thedykeneuk.co.uk/

You will be walking first on one section of old railway, then over fields and woods to return on a second section of railway line.

Start From the car park walk along the field line, turn right down the steps and you are on the Wannie line. Walk along the line until it divides and take the right-hand fork onto the Rothbury line. Continue on the line until you come to a finger-post pointing left down the embankment.

⓵ Drop down to the field and then through a gate to follow a path through the wood, which has now been felled. Continue alongside the burn, entering a section of wood that is still standing. As the burn bears to the right, exit the woods through a gate.

⓶ The route goes up the slope towards the gate that you can see on the skyline, but bear left of the gate because the route follows the line of the trees indicated by the arrows. The path bears away from the trees, where you go through a gate, and straight ahead you can see another gate. There are steps on the other side of the gate, leading you down a small rock face that was once part of a quarry. Turn left to walk past a pond on the quarry floor, and turn right on the track when you reach the wall line. At this point look back to your left to see the impressive set of lime kilns.

⓷ Continue on the track as it bears left to cross a minor road and head along the field line, with the bank to your right. Turn left at the end of the field and walk down to the farm road, then turn right towards the cottage at Low Fairnley. Turn left after the cottage, walk across the field, over a bridge and then over a double stile to the right of the farm gate. Continue along the field edge until you come to a wood, where there is a gate on the right of the wood.

④ At the end of the wood continue along the edge of a field, crossing another bridge, and then up the slope to a gate. The path continues between a wood and a field embankment and exits through a gate to cross one more bridge and then up to the Wannie line ahead of you. Turn left when you reach the line and continue along it, crossing two minor roads until you get back to the car park.

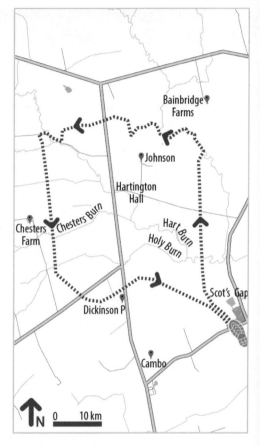

Points of interest

Wannie Line: The official name of this section of railway is the Wansbeck Valley Railway and it operated between Morpeth and Redesmouth, some 26 miles, between 1865 and 1963.

Rothbury Line: This section of the line operated between Scots Gap and Rothbury between 1870 and 1966. There was an intention to take the line all the way to Cornhill, but this never happened.

Yeavering Bell & the College Burn

START Car parking area next to
Kirknewton Activity Centre,
GR NT914302

NEAREST POSTCODE NE71 6XG

DISTANCE 6½ miles (10.5km)

SUMMARY Moderate/hard. A walk to
the best hill fort in Northumberland,
an attractive waterfall and the best
valley in the Cheviots

MAP OS Explorer OL16 The Cheviot
Hills

WHERE TO EAT AND DRINK Cafe
Maelmin, Milfield, www.
cafemaelmin.co.uk; there are
various cafés and pubs in Wooler

START From the parking area go out onto the B6351; the road is usually
quiet with minimal traffic. Turn right and walk along the road until you
reach a track on the right to Old Yeavering. Before turning right on the
track, take a moment to visit the early medieval settlement at Ad Gefrin,
which is on your left-hand side.

1 The sign at the beginning of the track indicates a public footpath to
Torleehouse (1 mile). Just before the footbridge that goes over the stream
there is a permissive path sign on the left indicating Yeavering Bell (¾
mile) next to the ladder stile. Go over the ladder stile,.

2 Stay on the track and it will bend to the left, then right to pass
the marker post that indicates that you are now on the Hill Fort Trail.
Continue along the track until you go over a ladder stile, then turn left
up the hill. The climb is quite steep, with marker posts indicating the
way; the track crosses the tumbled rocks that were once the outer wall
of this hill fort and brings you between the two tops of Yeavering Bell.
The one on your left is the slightly higher of the two and gives great
views of the countryside all the way to the coast.

3 From the higher of the two tops, turn left, heading downhill. Just
over the top there is a Y-junction in the track; take the right-hand fork.
The way down is easy going and towards the bottom you drop into a

gully to cross a small stream. Although there is a marker post on the other side of the stream, a path goes off on a right fork. Take the right fork and the path brings you to St Cuthbert's Way.

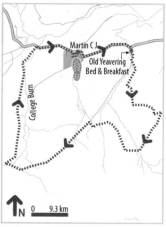

④ Turn right on the track and walk downhill until you reach a ladder stile on the left-hand side. Go over the stile and continue down the hill, going through a gate at the bottom. The path becomes a track, which you follow to meet a main track, where you turn left. The track will pass Torleehouse; go over a stile and through a small wood.

⑤ Just after passing the large stone sheep pen on your right, the track begins to bear diagonally right towards the tree line. It becomes a footpath, going through gorse and bracken thickets to bear left and then over a footbridge across the College Burn. Take time to visit the waterfalls of Hethpool Linn, before taking the footpath that goes to the right just beyond the footbridge.

⑥ The path begins to climb up the bank away from the College Burn. After a short climb the path contours round the hillside with the College Burn in the valley below to your right. Cross a ladder stile and follow the path now going downhill through a gate and getting closer to College Burn. As the burn swings away to your right climb a small rise, go through a wooden gate and turning right walk across the field to a ladder stile next to the road bridge. Turn right over the bridge and follow the road back to the parking area.

Points of interest

Yeavering Bell: Although there are other hill forts in the Cheviots, this is the biggest. The stone rubble stretches for 1,000yds around the circuit of the hill and would have made a wall as high as 9ft. All the stone was quarried from the hilltop and is an andesite rock, which when freshly dug would be a blue-grey colour. Some 125 hut sites have been identified inside the hill fort.

Guile Point & Return

Start Ross Sands parking area, GR NU131369

Postcode NNE70 7EN

Distance 7 miles (11.3km)

Summary Easy

Map OS Explorer 340 Holy Island & Bamburgh

Where to eat and drink There are various pubs and cafés in Bamburgh

This is a walk that is best done when the tide is out, as the walking is easiest on the firm sand close to the sea. The route goes north of Bamburgh to the navigational beacons of Guile Point and is one of those sections of beach that is rarely visited. There are often seals basking on the sand at Guile Point and, depending on the tide and movement of sand, remains of wrecks can be spotted.

Start From the parking area follow the signs along the road and through the sand dunes onto the beach. To the right you can see Bamburgh Castle and to the left is Lindisfarne Castle. Turn left and walk along the beach; providing the tide is out far enough, walk down to the firmer sand closer to the water.

1 Keep going along the beach, passing a large gap on your left between the sand dunes. As you get further round the point, the first of the two beacons starts to appear and then the second one comes into view. This is where you can often find large groups of seals basking on the beach.

2 The coastline of Holy Island looks close enough to walk to, especially if there is a particularly low tide, but do not be tempted – there are hidden dangers in the estuary, including stretches of quicksand.

3 Climb the sand dunes to get between the beacons. They are known as East Old Law and West Old Law; East Old Law is the one with the navigational beacon. Walk across to West Old Law and follow the track down to and along the beach, with the sand dunes on your left. The track gets firmer as you continue and makes its way through the gap between

the sand dunes that you passed earlier.

4 All you need to do is retrace your steps along the beach, looking out for the pole on the sand dunes that indicates the way back across the dunes to the parking area.

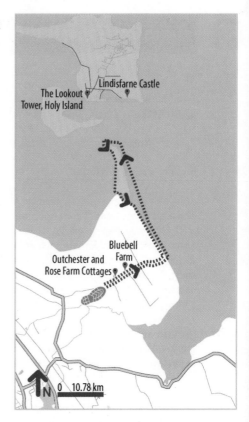

Guile Point beacons: These were erected in 1829 and replaced two wooden beacons. They are built of brick and originally had a wrought iron triangle mounted on the top. They are navigational beacons that were used to gain access to Holy Island harbour in daylight hours. Because of changing currents, which have altered the approach to the harbour, West Old Law beacon is not used anymore. Instead, a light was installed some way up East Old Law and a corresponding beacon has been installed on Heugh Hill on Holy Island.

69 Hartburn Glebe & the Wansbeck

START Hartburn car park, GR NZ089860

POSTCODE NE61 4JB

DISTANCE 7 miles (11.3km)

SUMMARY Easy; fields and farmland with a few minor roads

MAP OS Explorer 325 Morpeth & Blyth

WHERE TO EAT AND DRINK Dyke Neuk Inn on the B6343 road, http://thedykeneuk.co.uk/

START From the car park turn left onto the road, passing a left turn on a minor road, which you will take after visiting Hartburn Glebe. Pass the first entrance to Hartburn Glebe on your right, but turn right at the next entrance to the Glebe. At the Y-junction take the right-hand fork, which will lead you down to the Hart Burn.

[1] As you walk along the banks of the burn, you will come to the grotto on the right-hand side. It is worth taking time to explore this and be surprised at looking back through a tunnel when you get inside.

[2] Continue along the burn until the path leads up some stone steps until you come back out onto the road, where you turn left and walk back down to the T-junction. Turn right here and follow the road. Turn left at the next T-junction. The road sign indicates Angleton (1 mile).

[3] Walk along the road a short way to a public footpath sign on the left indicating Hospital Plantation. Turn right here, crossing the stile, and continue along the field edge. There are several fields to cross, each with a stile. The last is a wall stile over a tumbledown wall directly in line with the telegraph pole in the middle of the next field.

[4] The path exits onto a road at a bend and you continue straight ahead until you reach the T-junction, where you turn left. Continue on the road until it starts to bend to the left, where there is a sign on the right-hand side stating that the route is unsuitable for motors and indicates Highlaws (1 mile).

5   Turn right and walk down two fields until you reach a wood. Go through a gate, turn left through another gate and join a public bridleway, continuing across several fields, through gates and over the old Scots Gap to Morpeth railway until it reaches a minor road. Turn left here at the gate and then go through another gate a short distance along the road.

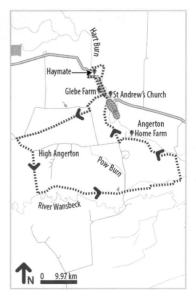

6   Head towards the group of trees that you can see at the far end of the field. Go through the gap in the fence line to the left of the trees and continue along the next field, keeping close to the wood on your left. Just after the wood there is a marker post indicating a left turn over a footbridge. Turn left here, keeping the fence line on your right; at the top of the field cross a stile to exit onto a minor road, where you turn left.

7   Walk along the road, passing the houses at High Angerton, and you will come to a public footpath sign on the right indicating Hartburn (¾ mile) just before the T-junction. Turn right on the footpath and follow it diagonally across the field. As Hartburn Bridge appears over to your right, take the right-hand fork and cross a footbridge over a stream, then bear right up the slope of the hill. The path exits onto the road where you turn left to the car park.

Points of interest

The grotto in Hartburn Glebe was cut into a natural cave by Dr John Sharp, an Archdeacon of Northumberland, who was vicar of Hartburn from 1749 to 1796. The grotto consists of two compartments, the first of which contains a fireplace. Outside, above the entrance, are two niches which once held statues of Adam and Eve. From the grotto there is a short slab-roofed tunnel that allowed ladies to reach the river, which is deep enough to swim in at this point.

The Five Kings

Start Holystone Forestry car park, GR NT950025

Nearest postcode DH8 9SS

Distance 7 miles (11.3km)

Summary Strenuous, especially the second part of the walk

Map OS Explorer OL16 The Cheviot Hills

Where to eat and drink The Cross Keys Inn, Thropton, T01669-620362; The Three Wheat Heads Inn, Thropton, www.threewheatheads. co.uk; there are also more pubs and cafés in Rothbury

From Holystone the walk to the Five Kings is on road, pasture and track. After leaving the Five Kings, the remainder of the route is over rough ground and, while there are marker posts and stiles, the tracks are non-existent. This is a route for map, compass and GPS if available. The views, though, make it all worthwhile.

Start Walk down the road back towards Holystone village, passing on the way a public footpath sign to Craig, which is the return route. As the road bends to the left, turn right along a track that leads to the gate of St Mary's Church, which is worth a visit. Continue past the church gate, turning right and then left to come out on the minor road.

① Turn right and continue along the road until you come to a public footpath sign on your right that indicates Dueshill (½ mile). Go over the stile and continue diagonally left across the pasture land, crossing several stiles and heading towards the trees in front of you. As you approach the strip wood, there are a number of stiles to choose from. Go over the stile to your right and, with the wood on your left-hand side, continue to the end of the wood where you turn left and then right through gates, following the public footpath markers.

② As you walk down the track, after leaving Dueshill Farm look for the marker post on the right indicating the way along a grassy track. Go through a gate, follow the track as it turns to the left and starts to go uphill. The track curves left and continues through another gate. As you approach the wood you can see the stones of the Five Kings in front of you.

3 Go past the Five Kings and over the stile to follow a path through the woods. You will come to another stile, which you cross, and then turn right, keeping the wood on your right-hand side until it ends. The direction is generally towards the tops of the trees in front of you. As you get closer to the trees, keep them on your left-hand side and you should see a marker post and then a footbridge. Cross the footbridge and you will see a marker post to your right. Take the indicated turn to your right and follow the track down and across the ford. After crossing the ford turn left to go over a stile by a locked gate. After crossing the stile cross a small burn, turn right and make your way uphill until you come to the circular sheepfold, where you turn left to come out through a gate onto a minor road.

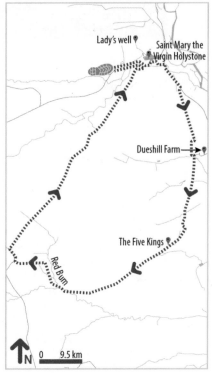

4 Turn right and walk along the road to the public footpath sign indicating Holystone (2 miles). Turn right to follow a route that lies on the high ground to the left of the group of trees that you can see ahead. As you reach the top of the hill there is a marker post and ahead you will see a stile over a fence that you need to cross.

5 Once over the stile you are on Holystone Common, with no real path to indicate the way. Generally it is downhill, and there are several stiles to cross that are often easy to spot on the fence lines in front of you. In summer the bracken is quite thick and high, so be prepared to spend some time making your way over it.

6 You will see Holystone coming into view as you descend. There is a path leading down to the footbridge, which you cross to exit through a gate onto the road. Turn left and make your way back to the car park.

Allendale Town, Catton & the River East Allen

START Allendale Town main square, GR NY838558

POSTCODE NE47 9BJ

DISTANCE 7½ miles (12km)

SUMMARY Moderate; riverside paths, undulating farmland and minor roads

MAP OS Explorer OL43 Hadrian's Wall

WHERE TO EAT AND DRINK There are various pubs and cafés in Allendale Town, including small speciality shops

START Keep to the right of the town square and head downhill on the road that leads past the Allendale Inn. As the road bears left, take the track on the right signposted Allendale Bridge. This will lead down to the footpath next to the River East Allen. On this section of the walk you will pass a tunnel called the Blackett Level.

1 Continue along the footpath and once the bridge is reached cross straight over and continue along the path until the fencing of the sewage works is reached. Turn right here and follow the path uphill, passing through a cutting of the disused railway. Immediately after the cutting turn left and cross a stile signposted to Catton. This track only continues a short way before bearing right over a footbridge and then uphill and over a ladder stile.

2 Head diagonally left to a gate that will lead you into the village of Catton. Cross the village green and up the road till you reach a minor road bearing left signed to Staward. Follow the road past the farm of Half Acres on your left and you will reach a ladder stile on the right-hand side of the road. Go over the stile and follow the wall on your right till you reach a gate in the corner of the field. Go through the gate and continue close to the wall, crossing two fields and going through two gates. The last gate is very close to the B6295; do not go onto the road, but instead go diagonally left across the field as indicated by the marker on the ladder stile to your right. Cross one more field by way of a ladder stile, reaching a minor road, and turn left uphill towards the

transmission towers of Catton Beacon that you can see over to your right.

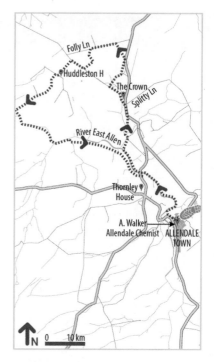

(3)   As you reach Folly Farm look for a gap on your left between the farmhouse and the next building. At the end of the gap there is a gate with a 'please close the gate' notice. Walk through the gate; diagonally right across the yard there is a stile over a fence. Walk down the field to the bottom right corner and over a ladder stile. Keep the wall on your right and you will see a small gate leading into the garden of Huds Riding. This is a right of way and leads down a lane to the road.

(4)   Turn right on the road and then left at the next road junction signed Old Town. Follow the road, turning right at the T-junction and then left, going more steeply downhill past Old Town, through a cutting of the same disused railway you passed earlier and over a fine two-arched stone bridge across the river.

(5)   Turn left at the sign for Allendale and follow the footpath past Oakpool Farm, keeping the river close to your left-hand side all the way to Allendale Bridge. Cross the bridge, turn right and retrace your footsteps back along the path back to Allendale Town.

Points of interest

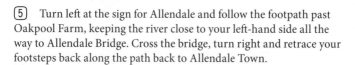

Before crossing the Allendale Bridge on the return journey, take some time to visit Allen Mill. Not only does this contain Allendale Brewery, but the site is a Scheduled Ancient Monument that contains the remains of the smelting works that made Allendale famous for lead and silver production in the nineteenth century.

Alwinton & Kidlandlee

START Alwinton car park, GR NT919063

POSTCODE NE65 7BQ

DISTANCE 7½ miles (12km)

SUMMARY Moderate

MAP OS Explorer OL16 The Cheviot Hills

WHERE TO EAT AND DRINK Rose and Thistle Public House, Alwinton, www.roseandthistlealwinton.com

A steady climb on the first section of Clennell Street to Wholehope, then on towards Kidlandlee through a forest, before another climb out of the River Alwin valley to rejoin Clennell Street for the return to Alwinton.

START From the car park turn left on the minor road and cross the footbridge beyond the village green. Turn left after the bridge and continue along Clennell Street past the farm, going steadily uphill. The track continues close to a fence line on your right-hand side, going through several gates including one just in front of a wood. Go through the gate and bear diagonally right to connect with another track, although this is still Clennell Street.

[1] Go past the sheep pens on your left and continue on to the ruin of Wholehope, which used to be a Youth Hostel during the 1950s. Go past Wholehope and walk up a grassy slope to meet a well-defined stone track. Turn right and follow the track into what remains of Kidlandlee Forest. As the track swings to the right there is a cleared area, with a marker post on the left-hand side.

[2] Turn left and follow the path until you reach a cross track; on the opposite side of the track in the cleared area is a marker post, which you head towards. There used to be a path through the woods, but the path although indistinct has marker posts that will lead you towards a gap in a wall, where you turn right with a wall on your right and head towards the buildings of Kidlandlee. At the end of the wall turn right along a fence line to cross a stile onto a stone track. Go through the gate opposite and turn immediately right to a stile, which you cross, and then turn left to head downhill away from Kidlandlee.

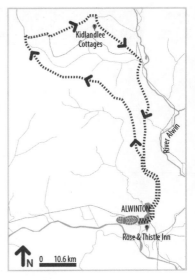

3 As you walk down this track you will come to a Y-junction, with a track to your right and the main track continuing on downhill. On the left is a path you will take past a clearing, which leads on through the woods. The area around the lawn is currently being cleared of trees, so the path may alter from that described.

4 The forest path heads downhill and comes out above a stony track, which bends sharply downhill to the left. Cross the track and you will see that the path continues down some cut steps to the bottom of the hill.

5 At the bottom of the hill cross the cattle grid and to your right is a public bridleway indicating Alwinton (2½ miles). Turn right here and climb the hillside, where there is a marker post at the top. Although there are a number of paths at the top, go diagonally left, following the contours of the hillside and gradually moving away from the valley you have just climbed out of.

6 You will come to the first of two gates that you go through to reach Clennell Street again, where you turn left to follow the outward journey back to Alwinton.

Points of interest

Wholehope: This used to be a very popular Youth Hostel during the 1950s; it closed about 1966. In the summer it was a destination for many walkers and in winter people came here to ski.

Kidlandlee: Look at Kidlandlee now and in the forest you can see several small occupied buildings. Had you looked this way in 1900 you would only have seen a huge shooting lodge up on the hillside. The lodge went through several owners but was eventually demolished in 1956; only the stables, kennels and croquet lawn remain of the original structure.

Clennell & Puncherton

START Clennell Hall, GR NY838558

POSTCODE NE65 7BG

DISTANCE 7½ miles (12km)

SUMMARY Moderate. A walk along the valleys and hills on the southern fringes of the Cheviots

MAP OS Explorer OL16 The Cheviot Hills

WHERE TO EAT AND DRINK Clennell Hall Country House, Clennell, www.clennellhallcountryhouse. com; Rose and Thistle Public House, Alwinton, www. roseandthistlealwinton.com

Initially following the River Alwin, the route heads east along a deep valley before climbing over hills to Old Rookland and Puncherton. It returns south to Biddlestone Chapel and back to Clennell along the edge of the National Park.

START From the parking area walk out of Clennell Hall on the track and turn right to follow a minor road past the footbridge on your left and the farm buildings on your right. After the second bridge go over the cattle grid and turn right on the public footpath that indicates Old Rookland (1 mile) and Puncherton (1¾ miles).

1 The footpath continues along the side of a stream called Rookland Sike in the valley bottom. When you come to a fence line with a gate, the path starts to climb the hillside away from the stream. As you climb the hillside, some trees come into view followed by the derelict farm of Old Rookland.

2 Continue on the path, through a gate in front of the farm, and then bear left heading towards a fence line and gate. Go through the gate and turn right to follow the fence line further up the hillside, passing a stile on your right. As the fence line bears away right, follow a path going diagonally left across the fellside. The path is sometimes indistinct but you are heading downhill into a valley. As you clear a rise you will see Puncherton on the hillside on the other side of the valley. Head downhill in the direction of Puncherton to go through a gate with a short climb on the other side, then turn right past the farmhouse.

③ Continue on the track a short way, looking for a path on your right that leads up to a ladder stile over a wall. Bear right after the ladder stile on a path leading up the hillside to a gate. Go through the gate and follow the path leading past a marker post. Just before the fence line the path bears to the right, heading towards a marker post that you can see on the skyline.

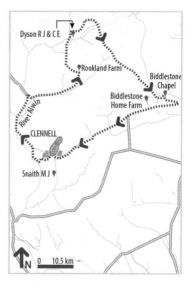

④ From the marker post follow the path until it comes out on the farm track, and turn left. Go through a gate and look for a public footpath marker post indicating a footpath leading left of the farm track and going up a hillside. The path goes over the top of the hill and down past a wood on your right to a gate at Biddlestone Cottages. Further down the path there is another public footpath marker post indicating a path to your left. The path is just before the wood and there is a barn on your right-hand side.

⑤ Follow the path through the woods and you will come to Biddlestone Chapel. From the Chapel head across the clearing to follow a track that leads to a minor road. As you turn right on the road look for a permissive path that leads to Selby's Graves. If you have visited the graves return to the road and continue along it until it turns sharp left. Ahead is a public bridleway that leads back to Clennell in 1¾ miles. You will go through several gates and a wood and then the caravans at Clennell will come into view. There is a gate on the left that you go through, then follow the path back to the car park.

Points of interest

Biddlestone Chapel: The building is a redundant Roman Catholic chapel that was once attached to Biddlestone Hall, which was the home of the Selby family until 1918, when it was sold. The hall was demolished in 1957.

Start Junction of B6346 and minor road heading north, Eglingham, GR NU105195

Nearest Postcode NE66 2DU

Distance 7½ miles (12km)

Summary Moderate

Map OS Explorer 332 Alnwick & Amble

Where to eat and drink The Tankerville Arms, Eglingham, www.tankervillearms.com

Parking Eglingham village has several parking areas but no official car park. You can park on the side of the road, and there is a small parking area in the lane leading to the church, close to the start

The route is down as moderate, but there is a steady climb from the start all the way to the top of Cateran Hill and the paths can at times be indistinct. The terrain, depending on the time of year, can get boggy in places but the sense of isolation in this area gives it a special significance.

Start From the start, walk north up the minor road past the World War II pillbox and over the bridge. Continue through a gate and then on a track until you come to another gate with a cattle grid. Once through the gate turn left on an unmarked path through the heather. This path, if you stay on it, will take you to the wooded plantation you can see ahead. As you walk along the path a fence line and a gate will come into view; the gate is to the left of the plantation and you should head towards it. A path does go to the gate, but it can be difficult to see among the heather.

1 Go through the gate. You will pass several cairns as you walk this path, but, before it goes downhill, diverge right to visit the Cateran Hole. The hole is located at grid reference NU102236 and from the path it is almost in line with the mast that you can see to your right. Then continue down the hillside to a T-junction, where you turn left onto a much wider track marked with a bridleway sign.

2 Keep walking along the track until you come to the ruin of Blawearie. From the ruins go straight ahead to a marker post, which

points to a bridleway that continues ahead and one that is going diagonally left. Ignore both of these and turn left on the path. This path goes straight ahead on a small ridge between the high ground of Grey Mare's Crag on your left and Tick Law on your right. The path descends the high ground and comes to a fence line and gate; go through the gate and follow the path to the left through the gorse bushes.

3　As you pass the last of the bushes, turn right on a path that passes through an old wall line and continues across the field. The path changes direction towards a footbridge over a stream; there is even a marker on the bridge.

4　After the footbridge the ground rises and you pass another hidden pillbox on your right-hand side. The path crosses another smaller stream and climbs to a fence line, where you turn right and follow it until you meet a wall line and can see Harehope Farm in front of you. Follow the wall line until you reach a gate on your left, which you go through, and then follow the track down to the farm.

5　From the farm go straight down the farm track, and as it bends to the right turn left on a public footpath that will lead down to the Eglingham road. When you reach the road, turn left and walk into Eglingham.

Points of interest

Cateran Hole: This is a cave that extends about 50yds. You can walk most of it without bending, but the last few yards are a crawl under a dropstone.

Blawearie: Now a derelict farm, a shepherd's family lived here certainly up to 1940, when the area was taken over by the military as a training and defensive area, which included a line of pillboxes running from Alnwick to Wooler. Wander across to the large rocks and you will find odd little garden areas laid out, and it is easy to imagine the family working there.

Etal & the River Till

START Etal village car park,
GR NT925392

NEAREST POSTCODE TD12 4TN

DISTANCE 7½ miles (12km)

SUMMARY Easy. A walk along the
River Till returning via Tiptoe and
farmland to rejoin the outward route
at Tindal

MAP OS Explorer 339 Kelso,
Coldstream & Lower Tweed Valley

WHERE TO EAT AND DRINK The
Lavender Tearooms, Etal, www.
thelavendertearooms.org.uk (open
daily); The Black Bull, Etal, T01890-
820200

An easy walk along one of the nicest rivers in Northumberland, the River Till.
The route returns along permissive paths and footpaths that lead in a long
loop back to the river across flat farmland.

START Walk to the front of the castle, turn left and walk down the
slope towards the river. Go through the gate next to the joint public
bridleway/footpath sign indicating Tindal House (1½ miles) and Twizel
Bridge (5½ miles).

1 Continue on a broad path alongside the river, turning left at
a Y-junction with a footpath sign to Tiptoe and Twizel. At the next
Y-junction turn right to follow the path up the slope to the gate. Go
through the gate and continue up the slope, turning left towards the stone
barn. In the corner of the field there is a gate between the fence line and
the wall of the building. Go through the gate and follow the path behind
the building and then out and along the field edge above the river.

2 The path continues along the field edges until you go over a ladder
stile and down the bank to rejoin the riverside path. It passes numbered
fishing positions and reaches another Y-junction, where you turn left to
follow the route past more numbered fishing positions.

3 The path comes to a sign that indicates that the riverbank path has
eroded and to use the higher path. Turn right, away from the river, on

the wide stony track and follow it up to the public footpath sign that indicates Twizel Bridge (1¾ miles). Ignore the sign and go straight ahead on the grassy track between the hedges.

4 At the T-junction turn right and walk down the minor road towards the farm at Tiptoe. At the T-junction turn left and then just after the farm take the left fork with a public footpath sign indicating Tindal House (1¼ miles). Turn right at the marker posts at the end of the first field and then through the broken gate at the end of the second field to follow the field edge alongside the next field.

5 When the path comes out on the minor road, go straight down the road towards Tindal House. As you walk past the farm there is a gate on the left-hand side with a public bridleway sign; go through the gate and turn right down the steep-sided bank towards the river. Once through the gate, you rejoin the footpath back to Etal and the car park.

Points of interest

Etal Castle: Built in the fourteenth century by Robert Manners as a stronghold in the Border Wars between England and Scotland, Etal Castle was captured briefly by the Scottish army prior to the Battle of Flodden in 1513. It gradually fell into disrepair over succeeding years and by 1603, when King James VI become ruler of both Scotland and England, it lost its military value and became privately owned. It is now managed by English Heritage.

Hartside & Little Dod

START Grass verge at Hartside,
GR NT976162

POSTCODE NE66 4LY

DISTANCE 7½ miles (12km)

SUMMARY Moderate. A journey into
the more remote parts of the Upper
Breamish valley

MAP OS Explorer OL16 The Cheviot
Hills

WHERE TO EAT AND DRINK Plough Inn,
Powburn, T01665-578769; Queens
Head, Glanton, T01665-578324;
Poachers Rest, Hedgeley Services,
T01665-578664

An easy walk to Alnhammoor but then uphill on minor paths until Salter's
Road. An easy downhill section is followed by a hill climb after leaving Low
Bleakhope. After leaving Hartside you could be on your own for the entire
walk.

START Walk down the minor road past Hartside and go through the gate
on your left signposted to Alnhammoor (½ mile). Go diagonally right
across the field to exit through a gate in the bottom right-hand corner of
the field. Walk down to the minor road, turn right and continue over a
bridge and up towards Alnhammoor.

[1] Just before the farm buildings there is a marker post on your right
indicating a left turn over a stile. Go over the stile and continue across
the field to exit through a gate, where you turn right. Stay on the high
ground above the burn until you go through a gate and start to descend
towards a stream and across a footbridge.

[2] There are marker posts indicating the way down the valley and the
grassy track starts to rise towards Little Dod. You will see a gate in the
fence on the skyline in front of you; go through the gate and continue
uphill with the grass track bending to the left. As you crest the hill there
is a Y-junction on the track; take the right-hand track and follow it
towards another gate that is ahead of you.

[3] Go through the gate and continue uphill. As you crest the hill

there is a marker post indicating the way straight ahead. Continue over rough ground to a waymarker and bear left to walk downhill, keeping a fence line to your left-hand side.

④ The track comes out through a gate onto Salter's Road, where you turn right. Continue down this road until you reach the farm at Low Bleakhope. Turn right on the road just past the farm and continue along the road, first through a steep-sided valley, and then the road will climb steadily before heading downhill back towards Alnhammoor. As you pass the farm buildings, pick up your original track and return to Hartside.

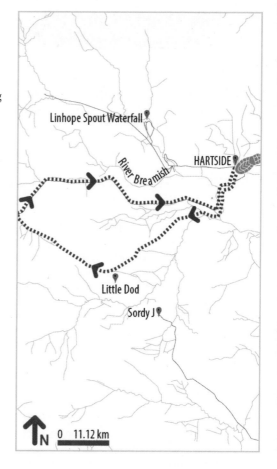

Points of interest

Four-horned Jacob's sheep are often seen along the roadside near Hartside Farm. The breed originally came from Palestine.

Hauxley & Amble

START Hadston Scurs car park (accessed from the minor road off the A1068), GR NU278007

DISTANCE 7½ miles (12km)

SUMMARY An easy walk to Amble and back

MAPS OS Explorer 325 Morpeth & Blyth and OS Explorer 332 Alnwick & Amble

WHERE TO EAT AND DRINK There are various pubs, cafés and fish and chip shops in Amble

The route follows a coastal track to Hauxley Nature Reserve, which is worth a visit, and reaches Amble by way of tracks and paths mainly across fields. The return is along a wonderful stretch of beach.

START Come out of the car park and turn left on the metalled track running alongside the beach, passing over a stream culvert that feeds onto the beach Continue along this track as it turns into a footpath and starts to bend round the right-hand side of Hauxley Nature Reserve. At the end of the nature reserve there is a sign pointing left for Low Hauxley. Turn left here and continue down the track to the entrance of the Nature Reserve on your left-hand side.

[1] Walk down another metalled track to your right, which comes out on a minor road. Follow the minor road as it curves left into High Hauxley, passing an information board on your right-hand side. Walk out of the village, turning right at the T-junction to walk down the road between Kirkwell Cottages. At the end of the road a sign indicates Amble in 1 mile. Go through the gate and along the field edge, turning left to exit on the minor road to Amble. Turn right and walk down the road into Amble. At the mini-roundabout turn left and then right onto Bridge St and left on Queen St, following the signs for the Tourist Information in Amble town square, where you will also find the toilets.

[2] Walk across the town square past the large sundial and turn right, heading for the harbour and passing fish and chip shops and signs for puffin cruises to Coquet Island. Walk right along the harbour wall, crossing the wooden boardwalk, and then right at the red and white

lighthouse. Walk up the steps in front of you and curve left on the path as it passes the now-derelict paddling pools. You then pick up the Coastal Path as it passes over the sand dunes, heading for what looks like a church steeple in front of you. The steeple turns out to be a rather ornate entrance to a cemetery, which you pass on the right-hand side.

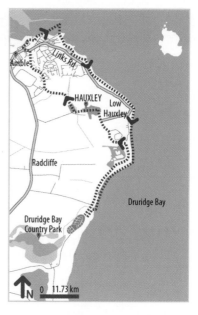

3 There is a combined path and track (the Coastal Path) that goes along the top of the sand dunes, but if the tide is out head down to the beach to walk back along one of the best stretches of beach in Northumberland. As you walk along the beach you will come to the large concrete stream outflow that you passed at the start of the walk. Walk off the beach here and the car park is just down the track. If you are on the Coastal Path, the path will bring you back to a sign pointing to Low Hauxley, where you retrace your steps to the car park.

Points of interest

Approximately 1½ miles from the car park you will come to the entrance of Hauxley Nature Reserve. If you have time, visit the new Visitor Centre and take a walk into the reserve. It is a haven for all types of birds at any time of the year and well worth seeing.

Amble grew from a small hamlet into a reasonable-sized town in the nineteenth century as rail links brought Northumberland coal down to the harbour for export. The harbour was the smallest of those that served the coalfields of Northumberland and Durham, but by 1969, with the closure of the freight rail line, these exports came to an end. Amble still survives with a small fishing and marine construction industry, and in summer large numbers of visitors enjoy Amble for its fishing trips by boat and the trip to Coquet Island to visit the large puffin colony.

78 Hethpool & the Border Ridge

Start Hethpool car park, GR NT893280

Nearset postcode NE71 6TW

Distance 7½ miles (12km)

Summary Moderate

Map OS Explorer OL16 The Cheviot Hills

Where to eat and drink Cafe Maelmin, Milfield, www.cafemaelmin.co.uk; there are also various cafés and pubs in Wooler

The College Valley is restricted by permit to 12 cars per day, so there is very little traffic on the first section of road. The route goes west through woodland to emerge before the farm at Throwupburn. From the farm there is a steady but easy climb to the Border Ridge, with a return along a section of St Cuthbert's Way.

Start From the parking area walk into the College Valley on the tarmac road. Go past the permissive path sign for Great Hetha and continue until you reach the public footpath sign pointing right that indicates Throwupburn (1 mile) and Border Ridge (2½ miles). Turn right and follow a wide footpath through the forest.

1️⃣ When the footpath comes out of the forest, go through the gate and follow the path down to the farm at Throwupburn. Just past the farmhouse go right through the gate and then almost immediately go left through two gates to follow the path up the hillside. Just before the end of the fence on your left, turn right on a grassy track leading higher up the hillside. The track winds up the hillside with deep valleys on the left and reaches a fence line with a gate in the corner.

2️⃣ Go through the gate and continue on the track further up the hillside. The track makes a swing to the left and heads towards a wall with a gate; the wall represents the border between England and Scotland. Go through the gate, ignore the signs for the Pennine Way, and turn right to follow the track alongside the wall.

3️⃣ Turn right at the marker for St Cuthbert's Way, through the gate welcoming you to England, and follow the markers for St Cuthbert's Way. The markers make the path easy to follow, but where it goes through a wood look for the markers on the trees. The path continues to Elsdonburn and winds down and to the right onto a minor road.

Continue on the road until you reach a T-junction, where you turn right to walk through Hethpool and back to the car park.

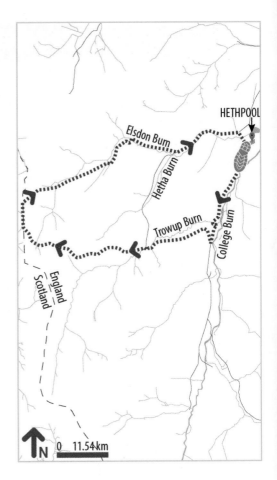

Humbleton Burn & Hellpath

Start Humbleton Burn picnic site, GR NT976272

Nearest postcode NE71 6RL

Distance 7½ miles (12km)

Summary Easy. An enjoyable walk into Cheviot country, not hilly and with fine views

Map OS Explorer OL16 The Cheviot Hills

Where to eat and drink There are various cafés and pubs in Wooler

An easy walk from the picnic site to a scenic valley using the Hellpath, which is probably a corruption of the word 'hill path', then a short climb to Commonburn House and an easy return along a main track.

Start Walk out of the car park, turn right on the road and walk to the finger-post that you can see on your left-hand side. The public bridleway sign indicates St Cuthbert's Way; turn left here and follow the path along the tree line to a gate. Go through the gate and continue uphill, following the path towards the cottages at Wooler Common. Walk past the rear of the cottages to a stile on your left, which you go over. Cross the field, go over a second stile and turn right. The public bridleway sign indicates Broadstruther (2¾ miles).

1 Continue along the track until you come to a Y-junction, where a marker post indicates a left turn down into the valley. Turn left and follow the track into the valley and along the burn until you come to a footbridge, which you cross. Turn right and continue along the path, passing through a gate after a short climb. After the gate you come to a marker post that indicates a turn away from the path to Broadstruther. Turn right and follow the path uphill, going past some grouse butts. Look out for the fence line coming in on the left-hand side, and you will see a marker post that indicates the path going almost alongside the fence line. A short way along the fence is a stile on the left that you go over to head diagonally right across the field.

2 As you get closer to Commonburn House you may be able to cross the ford; otherwise there is a footbridge on your right. Cross the bridge, turn left and follow the path up to the House. Turn right onto the road and continue along the well-defined track, passing the remote Bells Valley house down in the valley to your left. A short distance from Bells Valley you cross a cattle grid and the track changes to a minor road that will lead you back to the car park.

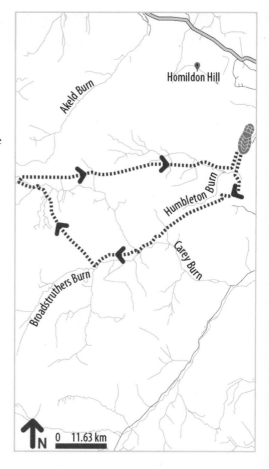

Points of interest

Watch Hill: The main hill in the centre of this route holds a central position in this part of the Cheviots. During the turbulent days of the Border troubles in the fifteenth and sixteenth centuries, the hill was used as a lookout post – hence the name.

Once Brewed & Vindolanda

START Once Brewed National Park Visitor Centre car park, GR NY752668

POSTCODE NE47 7AN

DISTANCE 7½ miles (12km)

SUMMARY Hard. One of the most scenic sections of Hadrian's Wall

MAP OS Explorer OL43 Hadrian's Wall

WHERE TO EAT AND DRINK There is a small refreshments area in the Visitor Centre shop (open Apr–end Oct); The Twice Brewed Inn is almost adjacent to the Visitor Centre on the B6318, To1434-344534, www.twicebrewedinn.co.uk

Starting from the Once Brewed car park, the route goes up to and along one of the most scenic sections of Hadrian's Wall to Housesteads Fort, before turning south and then west along the Stangate and past Vindolanda Fort.

START From the car park go left onto the minor road, cross the B6318 and head up a minor road almost opposite. As this road curves left, Peel Cottage is on your right and just beyond it also on the right is a gate. Go through the gate and pass through a second gate, turning right to follow the course of Hadrian's Wall.

1 The first section of the Wall is an ascent up Peel Crags and then there are a few more ascents and descents, one of which includes the famous Sycamore Gap, before reaching Highshield Crags, overlooking Crag Lough. The Wall descends to Hotbank Farm, before rising again to pass the intersection of the Pennine Way. As you go over a stile at Housesteads Crags, there is an opportunity to walk on top of the Wall until you reach Housesteads Fort.

2 Turn right through a gate at the closest corner of the fort and walk down the path towards the museum buildings that you can see ahead of you. Housesteads Visitor Information Centre is hidden behind the trees further down the track. At the junction of the track and an asphalt road leading away to your right, turn onto the road and head down to the B6318. Pass through a metal gate and almost opposite to the right is a ladder stile over a wall with a public bridleway sign pointing ahead.

Follow the well-defined track as it ascends a rise and reaches a waymarker pointing diagonally right towards a telegraph pole on the next rise. Pass two markers as you head downhill through two metal gates to the left of East Crindledykes Farm.

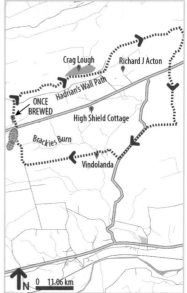

③ Follow the farm track away from the farm until it meets the minor road, where you turn right. Ignore the road leading off to your left and the next road on your right until you come to another road on your right, with a sign pointing the way to Vindolanda Fort. Follow this road as it bends left and passes two entrances into Vindolanda, the second entrance also being the main car park. Continue down the road, passing Causeway House, the only house in Northumberland thatched in heather.

④ The road continues on to a T-junction, but as you approach the junction keep looking right for a long-distance view of Sycamore Gap. Before turning right onto the road leading back to the Once Brewed car park, look ahead down the straight track and then behind you along the road. This was once part of the Stangate or Stone Road. This road was built in the early part of the Roman occupation and ran from Corbridge in the east to Carlisle in the west.

Points of interest

Vindolanda Fort, built on the route of the Stangate Road, was one of 13 forts that were staged along the road between Corbridge and Carlisle. Vindolanda was occupied for over 300 years and saw many re-builds as generations of soldiers were stationed here. The Stangate Road provided much of the foundation for the medieval Carelgate or Carlisle Road, but by the mid-eighteenth century it had became unusable by coaches and wagons, and the new Military Road, the B6318, was built between 1746 and 1752.

Steel Rigg & Housesteads

START Steel Rigg car park,
GR NY750676

NEAREST POSTCODE NE47 7AW

DISTANCE 7½ miles (12km)

SUMMARY Hard

MAP OS Explorer OL43 Hadrian's
Wall

WHERE TO EAT AND DRINK The Twice
Brewed Inn is on the B6318 close to
the car park, To1434-344534,
www.twicebrewedinn.co.uk

Starting from Steel Rigg car park, the route goes north of Hadrian's Wall
with great views of the Wall and crags to the south. On the return the route
passes Housesteads Fort and continues along the crags, keeping to the line
of the Wall back to Steel Rigg.

START From the car park go out onto the minor road, turn right and
walk along the road to the first public footpath sign on the right. You can
see the track going away to your right as you approach the footpath sign.
Cross the stile and follow the footpath through several fields, keeping
the line of the fence to your left. There are great views of the crags above
Crag Lough, and further along you can see Hotbank Crags. Another
finger-post points the way across an unmarked field and the track
appears to be heading toward the farm at Hotbank.

1   As you cross a ladder stile exiting the field system, turn left on the
farm track; going right will take you towards Hotbank Farm, which
you will see from the other side on your return. The farm track swings
uphill, passing a small wood on the right-hand side. Pass another
finger-post pointing the way further uphill and continue along the
track, passing a lime kiln on your left and heading for a group of trees
directly in front of you. As you approach the trees, go through the gate
into the wood, follow the path slightly right and out through the gate
on the other side. You are now heading over the field on an indistinct
track towards the gate that you can see over to the right. The gate, called
King's Wicket, cuts through Hadrian's Wall.

2   Turn right as you come through the gate and head along the Wall

towards Housesteads. As you come through a small wood, go over the stile and at the bottom of the slope turn right through a gate and head uphill on a track, which will take you past and to the north of Housesteads. At the top of the hill there is a gate to your left, which you can go through, then walk down to the Information Centre and buy a ticket that will give you access into Housesteads.

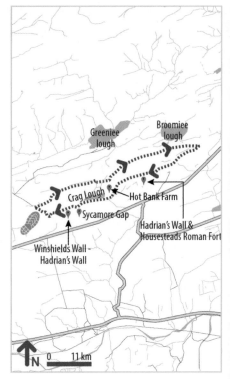

③ To continue the route you can walk along the top of the Wall for several hundred yards before coming down some steps and passing through a gate, keeping the Wall on your right. You will go over several ladder stiles as the Wall rises and falls along the crags that you saw on the northern side. At one place you will pass on your right a ladder stile with a finger-post indicating the route of the Pennine Way as it starts to head further north.

④ Pass the Pennine Way marker and continue up the hill on the pitched stone path. The path will come down past the farm at Hotbank that you passed on the far side earlier on the route. As you pass over the farm track there is a choice of paths to take. A gate on the right indicates Steel Rigg in 1½ miles. There is a sign to your left pointing to the Roman Military Way, which also indicates Steel Rigg in 1½ miles.

⑤ The Roman Military Way is a relatively flat track that passes south of the Wall, bypassing the climbs and descents that the path along the Wall makes. For the most enjoyable section, take the gate to the right, continuing along the Wall and eventually crossing it at the famous Sycamore Gap. The final descent is down Peel Crags and then up the grassy slope to follow the path back to the car park.

Haydon Bridge & the Stublick Chimney

START Haydon Bridge Station car park, GR NY842645

NEAREST POSTCODE NE47 6JZ

DISTANCE 8 miles (13km)

SUMMARY Moderate

MAP OS Explorer OL43 Hadrian's Wall

WHERE TO EAT AND DRINK There are various cafés, pubs and shops in Haydon Bridge

This route crosses the River South Tyne and climbs up to the high ground above the Tyne Valley. There are good views north towards the ridge, along which lies Hadrian's Wall; to the south is the Allendale Valley. The walk crosses the old Allendale railway line and goes as far as the Stublick Chimney, before heading back down into the valley via Langley Castle.

START From the car park turn left and walk along Church St to the T-junction. Cross the road and walk over the river, using the bridge. Turn left along John Martin St and at the end of the street turn right on Whittis Rd. At the top of the road turn left at the public footpath sign for Gee's Wood; the path leads down beside a wooden fence.

① Cross the footbridge and follow the path through the wood and under the Haydon Bridge bypass. The path comes out on the A686, which you cross to follow the minor road opposite. As you walk along the road, look for a gate on your left with a partially hidden public footpath sign indicating Elrington (1 mile). Go through the gate and follow the edge of the fields until you come close to a wood. Diagonally right is a gate that leads into the wood; go through the gate, over the footbridge and follow the path with the wall on your left-hand side.

② On reaching a small clearing, the path continues through the new plantation. Cross the stile on your right-hand side, then follow the path with the wall on your right, passing through another gate. As you follow the path across the field, start to bear right towards the farmhouse. When you come to the farm track in front of the farmhouse, turn right and follow it over a bridge and then at the Y-junction take the right-hand track.

[3] The track curves right into a wood and past a large house on your right. At the T-junction continue ahead, passing on your right-hand side the public footpath sign to Haydon Bridge. At the end of the tree-lined track go through the gate and turn left. There is a public footpath sign indicating Branchend (1 mile). Follow the path uphill to the old railway embankment, where you turn left slightly left onto a farm track, which will lead uphill to a gate. Keep going uphill, heading towards the roof and chimneys of Branchend that you can see ahead.

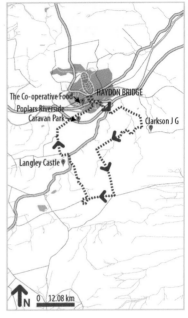

[4] As you approach the farm go through the gate, turn right on the road and take the right-hand turn at the Y-junction. Continue along the road past the public footpath on your right that you will use after visiting Stublick Chimney. The chimney is a short distance past the sign on the left-hand side of the road. After visiting the chimney with its information board, return to the public footpath, go through the gate and head downhill towards the farm cottage of Humbleton. Just past the cottage on the left-hand side go over the stile and follow the path along the contour of the hill.

[5] When you reach the fallen stones of an old wall, head downhill through the trees to cross a partially hidden stile the other side of a fallen wall. Follow the wall line on your right to cross a ladder stile and then across the railway cutting to make your way downhill on a grassy track to a wall stile that will lead into a wood. Follow the path downhill where it reaches a track and then to the A686 opposite Langley Castle.

[6] Turn right on the road and walk down to a minor road on your left to Castle Farm and then take the public byway straight ahead to West Land Ends. Turn right when you reach the minor road and right again at the T-junction. Follow the road all the way, going under the bypass again, past the caravan site and bearing left onto Shaftoe St, before turning left over the bridge and making your way back to the car park.

Lambley & the South Tyne Trail

START **Coanwood car park (South Tyne Trail), GR NY679595**

NEAREST POSTCODE **NE49 0QU**

DISTANCE **8 miles (13km)**

SUMMARY **Moderate. A mix of terrain from railway trail to high moorland**

MAP **OS Explorer OL43 Hadrian's Wall**

WHERE TO EAT AND DRINK **There are various cafés, pubs and shops in Haltwhistle**

The route follows the South Tyne Trail, before crossing the South Tyne River and climbing up to Lambley Common to follow the Pennine/Maiden Way to Burnstones. The last part of the walk goes over Lambley Viaduct, which opened in 1852 to carry rail transport high over the river.

START From the car park follow the footpath that continues on the opposite side of the road. Continue through the woods, passing the old platform of Coanwood Station, and turn right on the public right of way to Lambley Footbridge. At the bottom of the hill follow the path to the left of the house, cross the stream and walk behind the house diagonally across the field. As you approach the River South Tyne you will see a marker post; turn left and after crossing a stile make your way across the footbridge. You will come back over the viaduct.

① Turn left after crossing the river and climb the steps leading up from the river bank. At the four-way signpost turn right on the public footpath indicating Lambley (¼ mile). After climbing some more steps you will come to a gate; ignore this and turn right on a footpath that is high above the river. The path leads behind the cottages in Lambley and makes a left turn onto a minor road. Turn right almost immediately to follow a public footpath that leads to a tunnel under a minor road.

② Continue on the footpath across fields, passing to the right of a house. Turn left to cross the road and go over the stile next to the public footpath sign indicating Burnstones (3 miles). You are now on the Pennine/Maiden Way, which is part of an old Roman road that leads to the Roman fort of Whitley Castle near Alston. The first part of the footpath is uphill, but after the second stile the route starts to go downhill towards Glendue Burn.

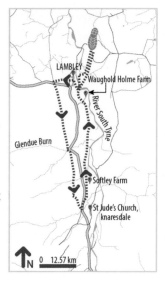

3   Before reaching the burn look for a wall stile on your right, which you cross. Turn left after crossing the stile and follow the path down beside the wall to cross first a stile and then a footbridge over the burn. Follow the path as it comes close to the road and then climbs up a bank and over a stile. Continue on the footpath until you reach a public footpath sign indicating the Pennine Way back the way you have come. Turn left on the farm track and follow it down to a gate on the left, which is a continuation of the public footpath that has been legally diverted. Go diagonally down the field to exit through a gate onto the A689.

4   Turn left on the road and walk along it a short way until you come to a small car park on your right. In the car park is a sign for the South Tyne Trail; turn left back in the direction of Lambley Viaduct. As you approach the viaduct the footpath moves away from the railway to the right. Follow the path down the steps; looking to the left you can see Lambley Station, which is now private property.

5   Go under the viaduct and then follow the path left to climb the steps onto the viaduct, which you cross. On the other side of the viaduct follow the South Tyne Way back to the car park.

Points of interest

Lambley Viaduct: The viaduct is on the route of the Alston to Haltwhistle railway line. Construction of the line was started in 1850 from both ends and a full service along all its length was started in 1852 on completion of the viaduct. This railway line has the distinction of being the longest serving branch line in rural north-east England, but declining numbers of passengers and better road links meant that the rail service eventually ceased in 1976.

Start Tourist Information Office, Morpeth, GR NZ200858

Postcode NE61 1PJ

Distance 8 miles (13km)

Summary Easy. Carlisle Park in Morpeth, riverside paths, country lanes and fields

Map OS Explorer 325 Morpeth & Blyth

Where to eat and drink There are various pubs and cafés in Morpeth

Parking Morpeth operate a free car park scheme with a 3-hour parking period, apart from Staithes Lane Long Stay car park, which is all day. The scheme uses parking disks, which can be purchased locally

Start The route starts at the Tourist Information Centre, which is next to the Morpeth Telford Bridge. Go to the right of the Information Office and cross the Chantry Footbridge over the River Wansbeck. The footbridge is named after the thirteenth-century chapel which now houses the Information Centre. Turn right after crossing the bridge and bear left, following the footpath uphill.

① Continue uphill then on the level for a short while until the path drops back down to reach the path alongside the river. Follow this riverside path until it comes out on the B6343. Walk on the pavement on the left side of the road to meet a footpath on the left signed to Mitford. Follow the footpath until it meets a minor road and turn left. You will meet this minor road again on your return. Just after the left turn there is a track on the right leading into a wood; a sign indicates Mitford (1½ miles). Turn left at the main track junction close to the river; a second sign now indicates Mitford (1 mile).

② Continue on the main track, following the course of the river to your right. The track gradually climbs and passes beneath the main A1 road bridge over the River Wansbeck. Climb over the stile on the other side of the bridge, turn right and walk along the field edge. The track continues down to cross a final stile, go over a footbridge and up towards Mitford

Bridge. From the bridge continue up the road to the T-junction and turn right left? on the B6343.

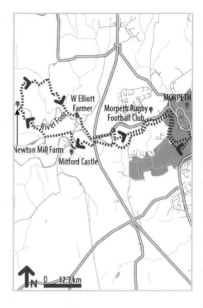

③ Continue along this road a short way until you reach the entrance to Mitford Hall on your left. Directly opposite, go over the stile and follow the track diagonally left, heading towards the house you will see across a second field. To the right of the house pass through a metal gate and follow the track past a copse of trees and along a field track. Turn right at the T-junction and continue down the track, turning right again before the farm. Just after turning right, cross a stile on your left that will take you across a footbridge over the River Font. Come out on the main track, turn left and walk up the track to reach a minor road at Newton Park. Turn right on this minor road and continue on until just before a sharp left turn, where there is a bridleway on your right signed Mitford (1 mile). Follow the bridleway as it bends to the left, but at the next fence line turn right and head towards the wood. Pass through a gate and start to walk down towards the river.

④ The track here is called Clarty Lonnen, which means a muddy track, and this one is steep and very muddy. To miss the worst of it move across to the left-hand side and come down on the high ground above the lonnen. At the bottom go through the gate and follow the track past a farm. If the river over the ford is too high, head left and pass through a gate that will lead you down to the B6343 to the left of the river. If you have managed to cross the ford, walk down the track and come out on the road to the right of the river. In either case turn left and walk out of Mitford on the left-hand side of the road. The road will go under the A1, and as it crosses the river and starts to bend left look for a gate on the right-hand side. Go through the gate and turn right to go through second gate, and follow the track almost alongside the river and close to an old weir. Just before the wood turn left along a straight track to meet the minor road that you came to on the way out. From here follow the track back into Morpeth.

85 Hulne Park Circular

START Ratten Row parking area, GR NU181137

NEAREST POSTCODE NE66 3HX

DISTANCE 8½ miles (13.7km)

SUMMARY An easy walk around the grounds of Hulne Park. The route visits Brizlee Tower and Hulne Priory

MAP OS Explorer 332 Alnwick & Amble

WHERE TO EAT AND DRINK There are various pubs and cafés in Alnwick

PARKING There is parking on the left-hand side of the road as you enter the Ratten Row parking area

Hulne Park is open to the public from 11am until sunset and its only public point of access is via the park entrance at the top of Ratten Row. The route follows two marked routes in the park, the blue route and the yellow route. The yellow route includes a short climb, at the top of which are good views of the countryside to the west of the park.

START From the parking area at Ratten Row head up the road towards the entrance to Hulne Park. Pass through the gates and onto Farm Dr, which bends to the right after a short way and over the bridge. Continue along Farm Dr through the open area and past Park Farm on your right. Turn left on the track marked with a yellow marker. As this track heads uphill, turn left at the T-junction and then right at the crossroads. As you head up the slope look out for the impressive gates on the right-hand side. The area enclosed by the gates and wall is going to be a cemetery for the present landowner.

1 The track swings to the right and passes Brizlee Tower on the left-hand side. After visiting the Tower, continue along the track and it will bring you back down to the Farm Dr/Farm Rd T-junction, where you turn left and continue along the road. You are following the blue markers along the road as it curves left and then right and passes the small holding at East Brizlee. Shortly after, you cross one bridge over the River Aln and then turn right over a second bridge across the Shipley Burn.

2 You are now on Palmstrother Dr, which will gradually work its

way down towards the River Aln. At the Iron Bridge bear left towards Hulne Priory, which is in front of you. As you approach the Priory climb the slope up to the gate set in the wall. The route goes to the right of the Priory wall, but take the opportunity to go in through the gate and visit it.

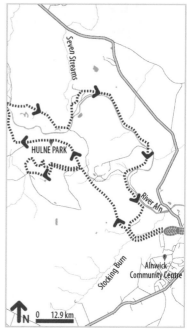

(3) From the Priory follow the path alongside the wall and out through the gate at the rear, then follow the track to the right downhill. Keep on the track as it leads down to the river and follow it along, with the river on your right. You are now on Lady's Well Dr, which will take you to a bridge over the weir. As you cross the bridge the track becomes Duchess's Dr, and you follow the track as it curves up and to the left into the wood.

(4) The track makes a sharp right turn and you might hear the noise of the sawmill up to your left. Continue on the track and it will bring you back to the Farm Dr junction, where you turn left to follow the road back to the entrance of the Hulne Park.

Points of interest

Brizlee Tower: The tower stands about 85ft high and was designed by Robert Adam in 1777 and erected in 1781 for Hugh Percy, 1st Duke of Northumberland, as a memorial to his wife, Elizabeth Percy, who died in 1776.

Hulne Priory: The Priory was founded in the mid-thirteenth century by Carmelite Friars, who thought that Brizlee Hill resembled Mount Carmel in the Holy Land. During the Dissolution of the Monasteries by Henry VIII, the Percy family took control of the Priory and it has remained in their hands ever since.

86 The Cheviot

START Car parking area, Harthope Valley, GR NT954225

NEAREST POSTCODE NE71 6RG

DISTANCE 8½ miles (13.7km)

SUMMARY Hard; a steady climb to the top of the highest hill in Northumberland

MAP OS Explorer OL16 The Cheviot Hills

WHERE TO EAT AND DRINK There are various cafés and pubs in Wooler

This route takes the easy ascent beside Harthope Burn as it climbs steadily to the head of the Harthope Valley. From there it is a short climb to reach the Pennine Way on Cairn Hill and then there is a paved section across the peat bogs to the trig point. The descent is easy, with good views all around.

START From the car parking area walk down the valley towards the farm at Langleeford. Go through the gate at the farm, passing the public footpath sign indicating Langleeford Hope (1¼ miles) and Harthope Linn (1¾ miles).

[1] The road now becomes a stony track all the way to Langleeford Hope. After crossing the ford just past the house, there is a stile on the left-hand side, which you cross to follow the Harthope Burn upstream towards the waterfall of Harthope Linn.

[2] The path continues steadily uphill, keeping close to the Harthope Burn. As you climb higher, the valley sides close in and the path crosses the burn many times before you reach the fence line at the head of the valley. Turn right to follow the path uphill as indicated on the marker post.

[3] Although this section looks steep, it only continues a short way until you crest the top and go over a stile onto the paved section of the Pennine Way. The sign indicates a right turn to the Cheviot summit (¾ mile). This section must have been difficult to walk before the paving was

laid, but even so there are places where some slabs seem to be slowly sinking into the peat.

4 The trig point, raised on a concrete base, soon comes into view but the Cheviot top is not one of those places to sit and look at the views. Continue on the paving past the trig point to cross a ladder stile, where the paving comes to an end. The path continues along the ridge past the large cairn, with the fence line on your left-hand side. As the path descends the views open out, including the deep valley that was part of the ascent.

5 The fence line turns away to the left as the path descends, but the path turns half-right back down towards the Harthope Valley. Go over

the stile and a little lower down through a gate to pick up a clearer path leading down to the road, where you turn left back to the parking area.

Thrunton Woods & Long Crag

START Thrunton Woods Forest car park, GR NU085097

NEAREST POSTCODE NE66 4RZ

DISTANCE 8½ miles (14.1km)

SUMMARY Moderate. A walk through woods and over fells and crags; once out of the main woodland there are views in all directions

MAP OS Explorer 332 Alnwick & Amble

WHERE TO EAT AND DRINK Thrunton Woods is off the main A697 road, to the north is Powburn (the Plough Inn) and south is Longframlington (The Granby Inn)

The walk climbs steadily towards Long Crag through woodland, which gives way to heather and bracken on the fellside and along the tops of crags. The views are extensive towards the Cheviots and Simonside and over the woods of Thrunton. Remember to look back on occasions to get a sense of distance on this walk.

START Take the wide forest track directly beside the information board and continue until you reach a T-junction, where you turn left. At the next T-junction carry straight ahead, and at the next T-junction turn right. The track descends downhill and at the next T-junction turn right.

1 As you walk along this section of track, watch for the footbridge on the left-hand side, which you cross. Go straight ahead on a forest path, which will start to climb through the trees. At the top of the climb the path swings left and levels out before coming to a T-junction. Turn right and start to climb again. Keep on this path, continuing to climb uphill and ignoring any other paths that turn away.

2 The path will level out and run along the contour at the top of the hill close beside Coe Crags. There is still some way to go before you come to the trig point on Long Crag, but as the track moves away from the crags it does come into view.

3 After leaving the trig point, the path starts to bend to the right and

descends the hillside. There are marker post at intervals on the way down; ignore the broad track that is off to your left. At the bottom of the hill the path comes close to the fence line on your left-hand side. Continue along the path until you come to a gate on your left, which you go through. The path leads on through the heather to the right, at times indistinctly, until you approach a stream, which you cross. Then turn left along another fence line, which is to your right.

4 This path leads out through the broken fence by a gate, but continues onwards between the fence line on your left and the tree line on your right. Before the trees end there is a gate on the left, which you go through, and then continue, following the path as it climbs the fellside and approaches a cairn. From

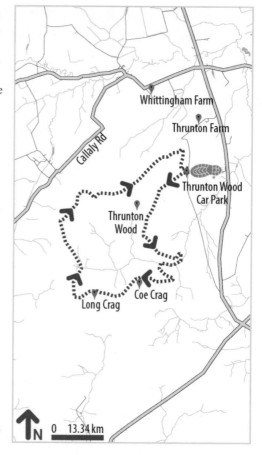

the cairn the path goes right and heads into trees and past a small pond on your right.

5 Leaving the pond, the path continues to a gate through a wall, where you turn right. At the T-junction turn left. The path widens out into a track, with Thrunton Crags on your left. Ignore the branch tracks to your right as you walk along, until the way ahead becomes narrower. Swing right on the track as it goes over the brow of the hill and then down to meet the main track you started on. Turn left and walk into the car park.

Blanchland & Slaley Forest

START Blanchland car park (£1 honesty box), GR NY964504

NEAREST POSTCODE DH8 9SS

DISTANCE 9 miles (14.5km)

SUMMARY Moderate. A walk across the moors to the north of Blanchland

MAPS OS Explorer OL43 Hadrian's Wall and OS Explorer 307 Consett & Derwent Reservoir

WHERE TO EAT AND DRINK The White Monk Tearoom, T01434-675044 (open daily 10.30am–5pm); Lord Crewe Arms, www.lordcrewearmsblanchland.co.uk

This walk uses the old drove road and packhorse trail around Blanchland and heads north to the start of Slaley Forest, before returning via moorland and the valley that separates Northumberland from Durham.

START From the car park walk out onto the minor road and turn left. As the minor road runs out, continue forward, passing the old mine workings at Shildon on your left-hand side. When you reach the last farm on your right, Pennypie House, go through the gate and bear right at the Y-junction, ignoring a finger-post indicating Burntshield Haugh to your left.

1️⃣ Continue on through a gate and then further on another gate, where you start to see the wood line ahead. At the marker post turn left towards a gate that is on the edge of the wood. Go through the gate and follow the track as it bears left between the trees. As the main track bears right, there is a track leading off to the left; the wood around this track has now been felled and you can see the gate leading out of the wood ahead of you.

2️⃣ After going through the gate, the track in front of you divides at a Y-junction. Take the left-hand track leading out across the moor. Go through a gate and continue on the Carriers Way, although the track becomes more of a path in many places. After another gate you can see the path begin to open out as you get closer to a shooter's hut and grouse butts.

3️⃣ The track leads up to and around the right-hand side of the hut and behind it and to the left there is a gate in the fence. The hut is usually left open and contains some tables and benches, which is very handy in bad weather. Go through the gate in the fence and follow the broad track as it curves right and then crosses the moor, before reaching a gate leading into a wooded area, part of which has been felled.

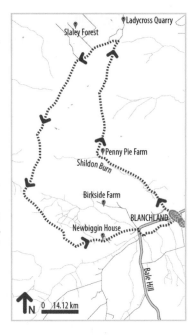

4 Go through the gate and follow the track round to the right. As the track straightens out, look for an unmarked path on your left that heads through part of the felled area. The path leads into a shallow trench, heading right and leading down towards a wall cornerthat turns left. Keeping the wall close on your left, follow the path down and past a marker post by a collapsed shed. Just after the marker post go through a gate on the left, turn right down the hill, through another gate and follow the track as it bears left to join another track at the bottom of the hill. Keep going forward on this track and on reaching the barns turn left; as you pass through a final gate the track turns into a minor road.

5 At the crossroads, turn right and just before the bridge turn left onto a public footpath indicating Blanchland (¾ mile) and Carrick (2½ miles). Follow the path all the way to the bridge at Blanchland, where you turn left and walk through the village to the car park.

Points of interest

Pennypie House: So called because it is thought that this was an inn on the drovers' road that sold pies to passers-by for a penny.

Carriers Way: Different from the drovers' road, this was a packhorse trail that went across the moors and made its way across to the mines at Allenheads. It would have been as busy as the drovers' road but without the wagons, sheep and cattle.

Blanchland Moor

Start Blanchland car park (£1 honesty box), GR NY964504

Nearest postcode DH8 9SS

Distance 9 miles (14.5km)

Summary Moderate. A walk across the moors to the north of Blanchland and back along the southern edge of Northumberland

Maps OS Explorer OL43 Hadrian's Wall and OS Explorer 307 Consett & Derwent Reservoir

Where to eat and drink The White Monk Tearoom, T01434-675044 (open daily 10.30am–5pm); Lord Crewe Arms, www.lordcrewearmsblanchland.co.uk

This walk uses the old drovers' road and packhorse trail around Blanchland, before returning via moorland and the valley that separates Northumberland and Durham.

Start From the car park walk out onto the minor road and turn left. As the minor road runs out continue forward, passing the old mine workings at Shildon on your left-hand side. When you reach the last farm on your right, Pennypie House, go through the gate and walk ahead to the finger-post indicating Burntshield Haugh that is slightly to your left.

① Follow the path across the moor and over a ladder stile on a wall; on the other side of the stile turn left and follow the path beside the wall until it comes to a T-junction. At the T-junction turn left through a gate and you are now on the Carriers Way. Ahead of you the path begins to open out as you get closer to a shooter's hut and grouse butts.

② The track leads up to and around the right-hand side of the hut and just beyond it and to the left there is a gate in the fence. The hut is usually left open and contains some tables and benches, which is very handy in bad weather. Do not go through the left-hand gate, but instead turn right and follow the broad track away from the gate.

③ After a short distance on this track you turn left on an unmarked path. If you pass a small quarry on the left on the main track, you have gone too far and need to turn back to pick up the path. Follow this path as it contours round the hillside and is occasionally overgrown and you will find yourself heading towards a large gully. There are quite a few paths here, all generally going in your direction, and you may find yourself higher up the hillside heading towards an old wall. If this is the case, just head down towards the gully as the path takes you round to the right and down into the gully. The path then crosses the gully at its narrowest point and climbs steeply up the far side.

④ At the top there is a marker post indicating the path straight ahead; continue forward, crossing a stile over a fence line. Turn left on the track and walk down to and through the gate, following the track as it bends left behind the trees. Go past the deserted farm of Riddlehamhope and keep going on the track over a wall stile and through several gates. There is one section where on the map the track passes though a wood, but the wood has now been felled. Keep going forward on this track and, on reaching the barns, turn left; as you pass through a final gate the track turns into a minor road.

⑤ At the crossroads, turn right and just before the bridge turn left onto a public footpath indicating Blanchland (¾ mile) and Carrick (2½ miles). Follow the path all the way to the bridge at Blanchland, where you turn left and walk through the village to the car park.

Points of interest

Drovers' road: Going north from Blanchland the track takes you along an old drovers' road that led across the moors to Hexham. As you get onto the moor you get an impression of the road's age just by looking at the depth between the road itself and the surrounding moorside.

Pennypie House: So called because it is thought that this was an inn on the drovers' road that sold pies to passers-by for a penny.

Carriers Way: Different from the drovers' road, this was a packhorse trail that went across the moors and made its way across to the mines at Allenheads. It would have been as busy as the drovers' road but without the wagons, sheep and cattle.

Bolam Lake & South Middleton

START Boathouse Wood car park, GR NZ083820

NEAREST POSTCODE NE20 0HE

DISTANCE 9 miles (14.5km)

SUMMARY An easy walk that visits some of the oldest features and places in Northumberland

MAP OS Explorer OL42 Kielder Water & Forest

WHERE TO EAT AND DRINK There is a café and visitor information centre in the Boathouse Wood car park (visitor centre and café open 10.30am–4.30pm weekends, Bank Holidays and school holidays Easter–Nov. Dec–Easter open from 10.30am but closes earlier at weekends and during school holidays)

PARKING Boathouse Wood, Low House Wood and West Wood. All car parks are in the confines of Bolam Lake (parking charges apply). In summer the main car park at Boathouse Wood is often full. However, there is usually parking available at the other two car parks. This route starts from the Boathouse Wood car park, but it is very easy to pick up from the other two car parks

A walk that goes from Bolam Lake to the Saxon and Norman church at Bolam, then down to the River Wansbeck and across ancient farmland to the medieval village of South Middleton and then a return through Shaftoe Crags.

START Walk from the car park onto the road, turn left and walk down to the T-junction, where you turn right. If you are parked in either of the other two car parks, you will have to make your way around the side of the lake to get to Boathouse Wood car park.

[1] As you walk along the road you will come to a sign for St Andrew's church. Turn left down the lane and into the churchyard through a

gate; a visit to the church will prove interesting. To the left of the church entrance is a gate, which you go through, turning right to follow a path down the hillside. As you walk down the field line you come to the farm at Angerton Steads. Follow the path past the tennis courts; there is a field gate on the right, which you go through, and continue down the field with the fence line now on your left.

2 When you reach the old Scots Gap to Morpeth railway line, go through the gates to walk along the field edge with the fence on your right. When you come to a gate at the field corner, do not go through it, but turn left to walk along the field edge and over a stile at the bottom of the field to exit onto a minor road. Follow the road round to the left and over the bridge across the River Wansbeck. Along this road a short way there is a gate on the left with a public bridleway sign indicating Middleton (2¼ miles).

3 Turn left on the bridleway and continue across several fields, re-crossing the old railway line where the bridleway comes close to the River Wansbeck. There is a footbridge on the left going over the river, but ignore it and continue along the field edge. The bridleway begins to move away from the river and crosses a small stone bridge over a stream. At this point you should turn left towards a gate that you can see across the field. There are now more fields to cross until you reach the farm track at Middleton Mill Farm. At the entrance to the farm go through a gate on your left to walk close beside the river, until the path leads you past the farmhouse and onto the farm road that leads down to the minor road, where you turn left.

4   Go past the site of the medieval village of South Middleton over Middleton Bridge, and turn right at the public footpath sign that indicates Capheaton (3 miles). Go straight ahead, clearing the edge of the old village, to cross a bridge over a stream. Go up the bank on the left-hand track and past a sheepfold that is in front of you, keeping close to the field edge on the left-hand side. Follow the field edge into the corner of the field, going through the left-hand gate to exit onto a track, where you turn right and then left after passing Middleton South.

5   Walk down the track and turn right to follow the wall line to the corner. Go diagonally left through a gate and across the field to pass a standing stone. Continue across the field to go over the wall stile and turn left along an old carriageway with the wall on your left and a line of trees on your right. This track will lead all the way up to and through Salter's Nick at Shaftoe Crags.

6   Follow the track up the incline through Salter's Nick, keeping the boundary wall to your left, pass through a gate, and continue to the crossroads where you turn right to walk down the minor road. When you reach a road on your right signed for Harnham, on the opposite side of the road is an access gate for Bolam Lakes. Go through the gate and turn right on the path to reach West Wood car park; continue along the path to return to either of the other car parks.

Points of interest

St Andrew's Church, Bolam: The church tower dates back to the late Saxon period, but the interior is largely Norman. It has an effigy of an English knight, Sir Robert de Reymes, lying in the church. Sir Robert acquired half of the barony of Bolam in 1295, fought in all of the Scottish wars of that period, probably including Bannockburn in 1314, and died in 1324.

South Middleton medieval village: First recorded in 1296, it was occupied until 1762 when it was recorded as deserted. The occupants were probably partly responsible for the huge amount of ridge and furrow ploughing that you will have noticed on crossing the fields. This was done by using heavy teams of oxen. Farming practices changed in the eighteenth century, which may have had something to do with the demise of the village.

Fourstones & the Scout Camp

START Lay-by north of Fourstones, GR NY888681

NEAREST POSTCODE NE47 5DG

DISTANCE 9 miles (14.5km)

SUMMARY Moderate

MAP OS Explorer OL43 Hadrian's Wall

WHERE TO EAT AND DRINK The Railway Inn, Fourstones, T01434-674711

Starting from Fourstones village, the route goes along the River South Tyne, then turns inland to climb to the Iron Age fort on Warden Hill.

START From the lay-by walk down the road to Fourstones, cross the road and take the minor road downhill, passing the Railway Inn, and cross the Tyne Valley Railway. At the riverside turn left and walk in front of the cottage through a gate and then along the path beside the River South Tyne. Continue along the path, crossing a stile over a wall. In winter you can go through a gate after crossing the stile and walk along the wall line, crossing a stile to rejoin the riverside path.

① The path will exit onto the road with Fourstones Paper Mill on your right; turn right and walk down the road past the mill. After a short walk along the road you will be able to walk along the pavement on one side of the road or the other. As you pass the first set of cottages on the left side of the road, there is a track between the cottages with a public bridleway sign indicating Fourstones (1¾ miles) and Whinney Hill (1¾ miles). Turn left here, cross the railway line and continue along the track. The track bears left alongside a wood and starts to climb a rise, heading towards another wood. In the corner of the wood is a gate with a sign indicating the bridleway alongside the wood.

② Ignore the sign and head diagonally right, aiming for another gate with a trig point to its right. Go through the gate and you are now on the Iron Age fort of Warden Hill. Go diagonally left over the fort to exit through an opening in the ditch walls, head straight towards the wood and pass through a gate along a track leading down through the wood. At the track junction turn right through a gate, passing a sign for

Fourstones and Whinney Hill. At the cottage turn left through another gate and continue down the track to a road, where you turn left; continue a short way, turning right onto another road at the T-junction.

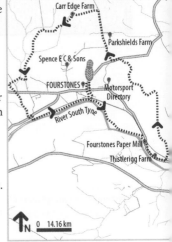

3 Just as the road starts to climb and bear left, turn left through a metal gate with a sign indicating Carr Edge Only (¾ mile). Walk up to the wood line. Pass through a gate and continue on the track through the wood. At the Y-junction take the right-hand path down to the edge of the wood through a gate. Turn left to Carr Edge Farm.

4 Pass to the left of the farm buildings, turn right past the farmhouse and continue down the farm track, which turns into a minor road, going past Newbrough Hall. Just past the hall and the farm cottages there is a footpath on the right between high hedges, with five stone steps leading up. Take the path to St Peter's Church, turning left through a gate after crossing a stone foot bridge. The path now leads beside a stream that you will follow to the River South Tyne.

5 After passing through some kissing gates, the path heads diagonally right towards a wall stile with a finger-post. Go over the stile, cross the minor road, go over another stile and continue on the path. After crossing another footbridge and going through a gate, turn left to walk alongside the fence line to a gate. Go through the gate and walk through a wood to a minor road. Turn left and then right before a road bridge onto a track signed to Allerwash and Allerwash Mill (½ mile). Cross the footbridge over the stream and turn right. At the Y-junction take the right-hand path that leads to an old weir and an information board. Walk alongside the stream until you come to a road, turn left on the road and then right on a public footpath signed to Fourstones (1 mile) and Warden Bridge End (3 miles). The path narrows and turns right, with the railway line close to your left-hand side. Go left under the railway bridge and left along the footpath beside the River South Tyne.

6 At the junction with the minor road turn left over the railway line, past the Railway Inn, over the road and back to the lay-by.

Wylam & Horsley

START Wylam car park, GR NZ118646

POSTCODE NE41 8EE

DISTANCE 9½ miles (15.3km)

SUMMARY Moderate; riverside paths, woodland tracks, undulating farmland and minor roads

MAP OS Explorer 316 Newcastle upon Tyne

WHERE TO EAT AND DRINK Boathouse Inn, Wylam, T01661-853431; Fox and Hounds, Wylam, T01661-853256; The White Swan, Ovingham, T01661-833188; Lion and Lamb, Horsley, http://lionlamb-horsley.co.uk

START The car park in Wylam is just behind the war memorial; from the back of the car park there is a main track, which forms part of the National Cycle Network Route 72. Turn left onto this track and past the sign for Ovingham (2 miles). Pass over the old railway bridge, Hagg Bank Bridge, and bear right following the signs for the Tyne Cycle Path. Continue on this path alongside the river, passing under Ovingham Bridge. Walk up the embankment to cross the separate pedestrian bridge into Ovingham.

1   Once across the bridge, enter the churchyard of St Mary the Virgin, pass by the church on the left-hand side and exit through the gate. Directly opposite is a stile leading into Whittle Dean. Follow the path with the houses close to your right-hand side, and continue on this path as the small stream, Whittle Burn, comes into view on the left. The path continues through the Dean, passing several wooden summer huts, and bears left at the three-way track junction.

2   Continue on past a footbridge and take the steps heading up the hill. Continue on the upward path and as it levels out bear left and go down a short flight of wooden steps, only to go back up a second set of steps moments later. The path turns into a concrete track at the end of the Dean. Bear right as it takes you over the A69 road on a pedestrian footbridge.

3   On the other side of the bridge bear right and then left to follow the track down a field, keeping the fence line to your left. Bear right at the bottom of the field and cross the footbridge over a stream. Head

diagonally right up the slope of the field and over the stile at the field boundary to enter a small wood. At the end of the wood cross two footbridges and go through a gate, bearing right to pass through a second gate and following the track to Spital Farm. Keep on the farm track until it reaches the minor road, where you turn right.

4   Continue on this road until you meet a track on the left-hand side just before a group of houses; it is signed for Horsley (1 mile). As you walk a short way down this track look out for the footpath that breaks from the track on the right-hand side. This footpath goes through scrubland and a small wood and comes to a gate at the bottom left of a wall. On passing through the gate, follow the now wide track as it curves right round the base of a small hill called Duns Law. Pass through a gate and take the path heading uphill, with the fence line on your right-hand side. The track goes down the incline and you have to re-cross the A69. Be careful here because you have to cross both sections of dual carriageway, passing between the central reservation barriers. Once across the A69 head down the path into Horsley and turn turn left at the road junction.

5   Walk all the way through Horsley until you reach the last house on the right-hand side of the road. Take the track signed Wylam (1½ miles). The track bends left and leads you between a wood and fence line. As you come down the hill and approach a wood, the track bears diagonally right and leads down to a stile. Go over the stile, and bear left around the field system to cross another stile on your left. Go across a footbridge and here the track goes straight over the field to a ladder stile.

6   Go over the ladder stile, turn left and walk to the edge of the field to cross a stile, before turning right to walk down the road into Wylam. Turn left at the T-junction and follow the road until you reach the Fox and Hounds pub. On the left is Route 72, which leads you back into the car park.

Allendale Town & the Chimneys

Start Allendale Town main square, GR NY838558

Postcode NE47 9BJ

Distance 10 miles (16km)

Summary Moderate

Map OS Explorer OL43 Hadrian's Wall

Where to eat and drink There are various pubs and cafés in Allendale Town, including small speciality shops

A walk that slowly climbs out of the Allendale Valley towards the valley of West Allen Dale, before approaching the chimneys from Dryburn Moor. The return route is downhill, with great views into the Allendale Valley.

Start Keep to the right of the town square and head downhill on the road that leads past the Allendale Inn. As the road bears left, take the track on the right signposted Allendale Bridge. This will lead down to the footpath next to the River East Allen.

1 Continue along the footpath until you reach the remains of a bridge; there is metal fencing overlooking the river at this point. The bridge originally crossed the river into Allendale Mill. When you reach the B6295, the entrance to the old Allendale Mill is on your left. The site now contains some small businesses, including the Allendale Brewery.

2 Cross the B6295 and continue along the footpath on the other side of the bridge. The footpath follows the line of the river until you cross a stile and pick up a farm track, which you follow towards the buildings ahead. At the buildings the track appears to head towards a gap in the wall, but there is a stile on the right that leads over the wall, through the gardens and down the left-hand side of the house, to exit through a gate and across a footbridge. Cross the field, go over a wall stile and another footbridge and turn left on the footpath heading uphill, which is signed as Isaac's Tea Trail.

3 At the T-junction turn right and then go over a stile and turn left across the field. Go over another stile, through a gate and head towards

the line of trees on your right that border a stream. In the corner of the field there is a stile that leads to a path through an avenue of fir trees. At the end of the trees turn left on the farm track and walk along to Keenley Chapel on your left-hand side. Continue along the road to the T-junction and turn left. As you walk down the road look out for the public footpath sign on your right-hand side that indicates Keenley Fell (1 mile).

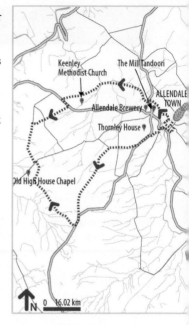

④ Cross the stile and stay close to the wall on your left-hand side. Cross two fields using the ladder stiles and go through the two gates at Keenleyfell East. Follow the farm track down to the minor road and go over it to cross a ladder stile on the opposite side. Head across the field towards Keenleyfell West, making a detour to your right to miss the boggy area. The path skirts the edge of the farm and exits onto a minor road, where you turn left. Continue along the road to the T-junction, turn left and then almost immediately right onto a public bridleway signed to Dryburn Moor (1¾ miles).

⑤ Continue on the bridleway as it curves around the hillside. On the last section there are frequent marker posts and at the last post you can see the road ahead. Walk up to the gate, but instead of exiting onto the road turn left on a path that keeps close to the fence line. Follow the path to the bridleway, which is leading left to the first of two chimneys. Ignore the track that leads away left, but follow a path down to the second chimney. Continue on the path, following the line of the flue until the path bends away left to rejoin the main track.

⑥ The track turns into a minor road and leads downhill past a crossroads, where another road joins from the right. Continue on the road to the next Y-junction, where you turn right, and follow this road to a T-junction. Turn right, cross the bridge and follow the road into Allendale.

Alwinton & Copper Snout

Start **Alwinton car park, GR NT919063**

Postcode **NE65 7BQ**

Distance **10 miles (16km)**

Summary **Moderate**

Map **OS Explorer OL43 Hadrian's Wall**

Where to eat and drink **Rose and Thistle Public House, Alwinton, www.roseandthistlealwinton.com**

Start From the car park turn left onto the road and follow it as it curves right out of Alwinton. Ignore the two left turns and cross two road bridges to turn right at a public footpath signed to Linbriggs (2¼ miles). Follow the path past the farm on your left and through a gate to follow the line of the River Coquet. The path moves away from the river and crosses a footbridge over a stream. Continue along the path, through a sliding gate, keeping the fence line to your left. Cross another stile and follow the path around the fence line, approaching two old cottages. Pass between the cottages and follow the path uphill; there are occasional marker posts indicating the way. Do not be tempted to head to the left towards the top of the hill. The second marker post is near a large tree, and as you contour round the hillside the third marker appears and beyond is a MoD warning sign.

[1] When you reach the warning sign turn left and follow the path uphill, keeping the fence line to your right. The path begins to head downhill, passing through a broken-down fence and across a stile, and heads through a new woodland plantation. At the bottom of the hill a finger-post points left, with the path following the course of the river. At one point the bankside has collapsed and it is necessary to work your way above this. When you reach the wall, cross a ladder stile to walk over the field, heading towards the farm at Linshiels. Walk past the farm to cross a stile in the corner of the field.

[2] Walk between the farm building to cross two bridges. After the second bridge turn left through a metal gate and follow the track round to the right, passing between the farm and farm buildings, through two

metal gates and out onto the road. Follow the road to your left until you reach a stile on your right signed to Shillmore (1¼ miles). A narrow path keeps to the contour around the hill with the river below. Stay on the higher path all round the contour and cross a stile. Ahead is a small copse of trees with a stile in front. Do not go down the hill to the obvious track past the sheep pens, otherwise you will have to climb back up again.

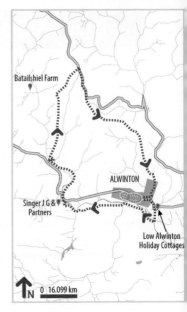

3 After crossing the stile at the tree line go through the copse over a stile at the far side and turn left down the slope. Pass through a gate and over a stream to follow a path at the base of a hill, with the river to your left. As you proceed along the path there is a small marker post on the right with an arrow pointing right. Take the track on the right, following the broad path uphill and then swinging left to head up the long slope of Copper Snout.

4 Follow the track uphill, turning left at a marker post some 20yds before the top of the hill. This left turn will bring you over the top and on level ground to a stile over a fence. Turn right here and continue along the fence line to a gate. Pass through the gate, and continue over some rough ground to reach Clennell Street.

5 Turn right on Clennell Street and continue until the stone track turns left. Ignore the left turn and continue straight on down a grassy slope; a marker post indicates the way. Go through two metal gates and past an old tin hut.

6 Keep following the main path as it swings around the rising ground of Uplaw Knowe. Ignore the track leading diagonally off to the left as the main track swings back to the right after going round Uplaw Knowe. Keep on the main track as it heads downhill onto a lane and comes out in Alwinton. Cross the small bridge over Hosedon Burn and turn right past the Rose and Thistle pub to walk back to the car park.

Bamburgh & Glororum

Start Links Road car park,
GR NU183348

Postcode NE69 7DF

Distance 10 miles (16km)

Summary Easy

Map OS Explorer 340 Holy Island &
Bamburgh

Where to eat and drink There are
various pubs and cafés in Bamburgh

From Bamburgh the route goes west along the coastline bordering Budle
Bay, before heading south-east along footpaths and minor roads to reach the
coast and returning along the beach to Bamburgh. This is an easy walk, with
a number footpaths and minor roads to make various shorter routes.

Start From the car park turn left, cross the road and follow the
path that leads below the castle and past the war memorial. The path
continues through the dunes onto the beach, but turn left to follow the
path indicated by the St Oswald's Way sign. Follow this path through the
dunes until it exits onto a minor road, where you turn right.

1 This road leads to the clubhouse of the golf course. When you reach
the end of the road continue along the edge of the golf course, following
the signs that still indicate you are on St Oswald's Way. As you leave the
golf course St Oswald's Way bears left, but ignore this and continue on
the public bridleway that will lead you down past some World War II
defences and start to climb away from the beach past a caravan site on
your left-hand side.

2 When you reach the minor road at Heather Cottages, follow it
a short way and as you reach the last caravan on the left turn right
through a gate and follow the footpath along the edge of a field. The
path leads down to a public footpath sign, where you turn left to head
diagonally across the field and exit through a gate onto the B1342. Turn
right and follow the road along the coastline towards Waren Mill. As
you approach the first house on the left at Waren Mill, turn left up the
minor road.

3 As the road enters the wood, look for a public footpath sign on the left indicating Drawkiln Hill. Turn left here and follow the path up the hill and through a gate, where the path leads past the old lime kiln on your right. Continue on the path until you reach a gate leading into a caravan site. Go through the gate but stay close to the fence line on your right and follow the path through another gate and onto a minor road.

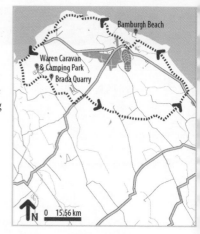

4 Turn right and continue on the road until the T-junction, where you turn left at the public footpath sign for Glororum (½ mile). As you follow this path and reach the corner of a fence line, the path should continue diagonally right across the field, just passing the corner of the caravan site. However, depending on the time of year, it may be necessary to continue along the field line, keeping the fence to your right, until you come to the road and then to turn left and follow the field line down to the gate.

5 At the crossroads in Glororum turn right and follow the minor road towards the farm at East Burton. Just after the farm look for a public footpath sign on the left indicating New Shoreston (1 mile); the sign could be hidden in the bushes by the side of the road. Turn left and follow the footpath across the fields, crossing several stiles and a minor road to exit onto a minor road over a stile.

6 There is a sign opposite the stile that indicates that the road opposite is a private road; follow it down past the farm at New Shoreston, where it bends left to come out at another minor road. Almost immediately opposite are two farm gates. Go through the left-hand gate and follow the field edge all the way to cross a lowered fence and the B1340, following the path down to the beach.

7 Turn left past the Monks House and follow the beach towards Bamburgh Castle. As you approach the castle look for a path in the dunes that will lead you up towards the left of the castle, and then follow the track down to the road into the car park.

Killhope Lead Mining Centre & Allenheads

START Killhope Lead Mining Centre, GR NY824431

POSTCODE DL13 1AR

DISTANCE 10 miles (16km)

SUMMARY Moderate/stenuous; roads and tracks crossing undulating moorland

MAP OS Explorer OL31 North Pennines

WHERE TO EAT AND DRINK Hemmel Café, Allenheads, www.thehemmelcafe. co.uk (closed Wed); Allenheads Inn, Allenheads, www.allenheadsinn. co.uk; Killhope Mill Café, www. killhope.org.uk (open Apr–end Oct)

PARKING At Killhope Mill car park

A moderate to strenuous walk on road and track from the Weardale Valley into the Allendale Valley and return.

START From the car park walk over the ford, cross the A689 and almost directly opposite is a gate with a public footpath sign. Go through the gate and head to the left uphill, following a path through what was once a wood. The path soon curves to the right, going steadily uphill with views opening below of the Lead Mining Centre. Once you come to a fence, look to the left and you will see a gate. Go through the gate and continue uphill, keeping to the left of a small stream. There is the occasional wooden marker to guide you along this rough path.

① The path curves to the right and at the top of the hill it reaches a wide track. Turn right and head downhill into the Allendale Valley. As you get further downhill, the track becomes more defined. This is the Carriers' Way, used among other things to bring ore from the Weardale mines for smelting at the mill that used to exist at the bottom of the track.

② At the bottom of the track turn right through the gate, go across the bridge over the River East Allen, and turn right along the road past the small number of cottages that make up Dirt Pot. Continue through the village and turning right up the hill on the B6295. Keep on the right-hand side of the road and head steadily uphill.

③ Just beyond the Northumberland County boundary sign there is a gate on the left-hand side of the road. Go through the gate and follow the path, keeping close to the wall, until you come to another gate, where you turn right and follow the track downhill, keeping the fence line on your right. The track gets more defined the further you go downhill, eventually passing Hollyhead Farm on your right. Just past the farm on the right is a well-defined track between low walls. There is no sign on this track but follow it to reach the B6295, cross the road and take another track to the A689.

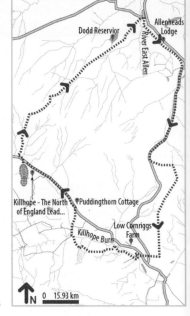

④ Cross this road and take the signed track down and across the river to Low Allers. Having passed through Low Allers, keep to the right-hand path and follow it to Heathery Bridge. Do not cross the bridge, but instead walk uphill and take the first track on your right. This track will take you past the farms of High Rush and Blakeley Field and across the unnamed bridge over Wellhope Burn.

⑤ Do not take the signed route to Killhope at the finger-post, but instead turn right to cross Killhopeburn Bridge. Just after crossing the bridge and before the road swings right uphill, take the track on the left going uphill. Although there are some markers on the track it can be difficult to follow, but generally head towards the gap in the wall you can see ahead and then finally through a gate to emerge on the A689. Follow the A698 back to Killhope.

Points of interest

Killhope Mine: This is a fully restored nineteenth-century Victorian lead mine, where you can experience for yourself the life and work of the lead mining families of the Pennine dales.

Tom Tallon's Crag

START Humbleton Burn picnic site,
GR NT976272

MAP OS Explorer OL16 The Cheviot
Hills

NEAREST POSTCODE NE71 6PB

WHERE TO EAT AND DRINK There are
various cafés and pubs in Wooler

DISTANCE 10 miles (16km)

SUMMARY Moderate/hard

A moderate walk around the lower slopes of Humbleton Hill on the edge of
the Cheviot Hills, with wide-ranging views.

START Walk out of the car park, turn right on the road and walk to the
finger-post that you can see on your left-hand side. The public bridleway
sign indicates St Cuthbert's Way; turn left here and follow the path
along the tree line to a gate. Go through the gate and continue uphill,
following the path towards the cottages at Wooler Common. Walk past
the rear of the cottages to a stile on your left, which you go over. Cross
the field, go over a second stile and turn right. The public bridleway sign
indicates Broadstruther (2¾ miles).

① Continue along the track until you come to a Y-junction, where
a marker post indicates a left turn down into the valley. Turn left and
follow the track into the valley and along the burn until you come to a
footbridge, which you cross. Turn right and continue along the path,
passing through a gate after a short climb. After the gate you come to
a marker post that indicates a right left? turn away from the path to
Broadstruther. Turn right and follow the path uphill, going past some
grouse butts. Look out for the fence line coming in on the left-hand
side, and you will see a marker post that indicates the path going almost
alongside the fence line. A short way along the fence is a stile on the left;
go over this and head diagonally right across the field.

② As you get closer to Commonburn House cross the bridge, turn
left and follow the path up to the House. Turn right onto the road and
after crossing the stream go through a gate on your left to pick up a

main track going over the hill. Continue straight ahead, ignoring any paths going off left or right, until you come to the waymarker indicating St Cuthbert's Way. Turn right here and continue on the path, passing Tom Tallon's Crag on your left-hand side. Follow the path down to a wood edge and turn left through the gate.

③ Continue down the track until you can see the farm of Gleadscleugh ahead of you. Just after the gate there is a track to your right, which leads down to a stream over Akeld Burn. Turn right, go over the burn and then zigzag up the hill and through a gate at the top.

④ Keeping the wall on your left, follow the bridleway around the side of Harehope Hill and then continue downhill through a gate, across a section of rough pasture and then through another gate. Shortly after passing the last gate, take the path to your right that leads up and into a narrow valley between Harehope Hill and Humbleton Hill. As the valley curves left into the ravine on the far side of Humbleton Hill, take the left-hand fork that leads to a stile and then the permissive path that leads upwards, with the ravine on your right-hand side.

⑤ A well-marked track leads down from the top to a gate, where you turn left onto a well-defined track. Go through a gate and just past an old railway wagon turn left through the gate. Go down the track, through yet another gate and head downhill through the wood. At the bottom of the hill push left through the trees and you will come out into the car park.

Cheviot Gravels
Akeld Manor House
Homildon Hill
Tom Tallon's Crag
Akeld Burn
Broadstruthers Burn
Carey Burn
N   0   16.04 km

Wark & Redesmouth

Start Wark village square,
GR NY861770

Nearest postcode NE48 3LG

Distance 10 miles (16km)

Summary Moderate

Maps OS Explorer OL42 Kielder
Water & Forest and OS Explorer
OL43 Hadrian's Wall

Where to eat and drink Battlesteads
Hotel and Restaurant, Wark,
www.battlesteads.com

Parking Parking is available close to
the village square; there is a small
car park on the other side of the
River North Tyne at GR NT863770

Start From the war memorial on the edge of the village square, walk down Main St in the direction of the River North Tyne. Cross Wark Bridge and turn left on the minor road signed for Birtley. Follow the road as it turns to the right up the hill and turn left at the T-junction.

① Turn right at the next T-junction; there is a sign pointing right beneath a tree indicating a footpath to High Carry House and Redesmouth. Go through the metal gate just before the road turns left, and on the left go through a wooden gate with a public footpath sign indicating High Carry House (¼ mile) and Redesmouth (2½ miles). Walk across the field in the direction of High Carry House; there is a marker on a telegraph pole and you will see the ladder stile over the wall to the right of the farm.

② Go over the ladder stile and turn right to follow the line of the wall. When the wall ends continue on with the fence line to your right. At the end of the fence line go through the metal gate in front of you and head diagonally left across the field, passing a stream on your left. Head towards the gate in the fence that is on the edge of a tree line. Go through the gate and down some steps to cross the railway line. Go up the steps on the other side and over the stile to drop down to the right towards the River North Tyne.

③ Follow the path through the woods to a field, cross the field, pass close to a house on your right and re-enter the wood through a gate. Continue through the woods, passing a wooden fishing hut. As the river starts to bend to the left the path climbs away from the river and leads to a ladder stile, which you go over, to come back onto the old railway line.

④ Turn left and follow the line into the remains of Redesmouth Station. This may be an adventurous part because the local farm sometimes lets cattle roam through the station and along the line, but you need to be on the right-hand side where the marker post points towards the cottages. Follow the footpath past the cottages and then down to the T-junction, where you turn right.

⑤ Walk along the road until it bends to the left, where there is a ladder stile on the right going over the wall. Go over the stile and across the field, over a stile and then towards a gate set in the wall. Keep the stream on your left as you go up the hill and go through the gate on your right to walk past Buteland on your right. Follow the farm road down the hill, and just after the metal gate turn right over the stile and across the field to a wall stile.

⑥ Follow an indistinct path down the hillside through the trees to cross a stream and then a stile on the opposite side. There is no bridge across the stream but it is usually fordable. Once over the stile, climb the steep bank and walk to the left beside the fence line. Go through the gate on your left and continue down the field, with the fence line now on your right, to go over a stile. Go around the marshy bit of ground in front of you and climb the hillside to the farm road. There are two roads that intersect at the Y-junction; walk down the main branch of the junction and at the T-junction turn right to the village of Birtley. As you leave the village and opposite St Giles Church, turn right on the public footpath that leads between two fences and then slightly left down the hill across a small stream and then up a bank to pass a wood on your left. The path goes through a metal gate onto the road, where you turn right to follow it down to Wark Bridge and back into Wark.

Warkworth & the River Aln

Start Birling Links car park,
GR NU254063

Distance 10½ miles (16.9km)

Summary Easy

Map OS Explorer 332 Alnwick &
Amble

Where to eat and drink There
are various pubs and cafés in
Warkworth

An easy walk along the River Coquet, along minor roads, through quiet
farmland, visiting Church Hill overlooking Alnmouth and the River Aln
estuary, before returning to Warkworth along the beach or sand dunes.

Start The route starts from the car park close to the beach, where there
are toilets. From the car park head onto the minor road and walk in the
direction of Warkworth. On reaching the T-junction go straight across
the road and walk over the fourteenth-century stone bridge, go through
the archway and turn right to walk along the river. As the road ends
continue on the track, passing a sign to Howlet Hall in ¾ mile.

① Before passing Howlet Hall you will come to the crossing point
on the river to Warkworth Hermitage. Take the track leading uphill
away from the river. Continue on the track and at the T-junction
turn right. This road changes into a track and as it curves left take the
footpath that is on the right, going downhill to cross a footbridge over
the river. After crossing, turn right to follow the track alongside the
river before crossing a stile into a caravan site.

② Go straight across the caravan site, heading uphill to exit the
site beside an old chain link gate. Turn left along the track to exit on a
minor road, where you turn right, cross the bridge over the railway and
continue until you come to a second T-junction with a public footpath
sign on the right indicating Eastfield Farm (1¼ miles). Go through the
gate and follow the unmade path close to the hedgerow until the end of
the field. Go over the fence on your left and walk down the fence line,
turning left at the end to cross over a stile.

③ Keeping the hedgerow to your left, follow the path until it curves right and crosses a stile to come out on a minor road. Turn left along the road and take the signed footpath on the right. This path curves left along the field edge, and a stile on the right will take you down some steps and over a footbridge. Head straight over the field and cross a fence line to the right of the garden. Turn right and then left across a field to a minor road. Turn right on this road and then left at the public bridleway sign indicating High Buston (1 mile). As the bridleway doglegs to the right, look out for a sign that takes you left, following the line of telegraph poles. After passing through a couple of gates, the bridleway goes straight up a field to High Buston at a stile leading out to a minor road.

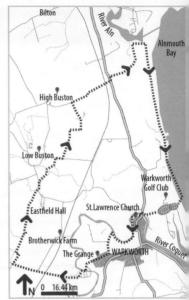

④ Turn right on the minor road and walk down to the main road (A1068). Cross this road and turn left onto a cycle and pedestrian path. Turn right at the bridleway sign indicating Buston Links (½ mile). Closer to the sand dunes the bridleway divides; take the left-hand fork heading towards the small hill and the ruins of a chapel.

⑤ Climb the hill to reach the wooden cross, then climb down to cross the open area between the hill and the sand dunes. To return to the car park you can either walk down the wide open beach or walk along the track (St Oswald's Way) that meanders above the dunes.

Points of interest

Warkworth is best known for its medieval castle, hermitage and church and has an easy riverside walk that takes in all three locations. At the far end of the walk and before returning to Warkworth there is Church Hill, once part of Alnmouth before a storm in 1806 put Church Hill on the other side of the River Aln. The cross on top of Church Hill is probably the site of a synod or church council meeting in the year 684, where St Cuthbert was elected Bishop of Lindisfarne.

Thropton & Tosson Hill

START Thropton Community Centre, GR NU026023

NEAREST POSTCODE NE65 7LT

DISTANCE 11½ miles (18.5km)

SUMMARY Strenuous; over farmland, through a nature reserve, up a hill, great views and an easy walk back

MAPS OS Explorer OL42 Kielder Water & Forest and OS Explorer 332 Alnwick & Amble

WHERE TO EAT AND DRINK The Cross Keys Inn, Thropton, To1669-620362; The Three Wheat Heads Inn, Thropton, www.threewheatheads. co.uk; there are also more pubs and cafés in Rothbury

Parking Thropton village has several parking areas but no official car park

This route is quite a long one compared to others in the book, but that's because the views are so good.

START The walk starts at the Community Centre, where there are parking spaces on the road. Just past the Community Centre there is a lane that goes down the right-hand side of the building. There is a public footpath sign on the left that indicates Ryehill (¾ mile). At the bottom of the lane turn left and then cross the footbridge and take the right-hand path.

① Cross the field to a gate and turn left through another gate. Turn right to walk along the edge of the field, with the fence on your right. At the end of the field go through a gate and turn right to walk down the track to a public bridleway sign that indicates Bickerton (2 miles). Cross the field to exit through a gate that leads between two small woods.

② Continue on the path, taking a left turn at the large bridlepath sign. This will lead you onto a track that has lakes on your right-hand side. Just before the end of the lake there is a stile on the left, which you cross, and then head diagonally right across the field to come out on the road at Bickerton. Turn right and continue along it until you come to the sign for Hepple Whitefield Farm. Go left down the farm track past the farm to cross a stile and then cross the field to exit through a gate, where you turn left on a minor road.

③ At the Y-junction there is a bridleway sign that points right along the edge of the tree line; this bridleway leads onto a track just past the house at Hepple Whitefield. Follow the track until the fence line on your left turns away, and then head diagonally left across the field. Pass through a gate.

④ Follow the track as it heads up the side of Whitefield Hill. Further up the track you will pass two shooting huts in a dip on your left-hand side. Beyond the huts on higher ground you will come to a grouse butt, also on your left. Just beyond the grouse butt there is a track on your left. Turn left here and follow the track across the heather as it climbs towards the trig point on the top of Tosson Hill.

⑤ From the trig point continue on a broader track until you come to a gate. Go through the gate and follow the path down to a main track. Keep on this until you reach the Simonside information board, and turn left at a marker post that leads down to a main track junction. On the left-hand side take the bridleway through the trees to come out on a main track, where you turn right. Follow the track for a short distance until you go through a gate on your left-hand side, taking you along the wood line to the right.

⑥ This track leads downhill to Great Tosson, where you cross a stile and turn right, walking past the cottages to the road, where you turn left. Keep on the road past Tosson Lime Kiln, and at the T-junction cross the field at the footpath sign that indicates Thropton (¾ mile). Follow the path across the fields. Cross the footbridge, and follow the path back to the Community Centre.